Our Syndromes,
Ourselves

Our *Syndromes,* Ourselves

CATHY HAMILTON

**Andrews McMeel
Publishing**

Kansas City

Our Syndromes, Ourselves

00 01 02 03 RDC 10 9 8 7 6 5 4 3 2 1

Library of Congress Cataloging-in-Publication Data
Hamilton, Cathy.
    Our syndromes, ourselves / by Cathy Hamilton.
        p.   cm.
    ISBN 0-7407-0665-9 (pbk.)
        1. Diseases in women—Popular works. 2. Syndromes—Popular
    works. 3. Women—Health and hygiene—Humor. I. Title.
RC48.6.H36 2000
616'.0082—dc21   99-044000

Design by Holly Camerlinck

To my family . . .

who loves me in spite
of my syndromes.

I love you back.

ACKNOWLEDGMENTS

Thanks to the folks at Andrews McMeel Publishing—
    especially Dorothy O'Brien;
my mother, Mignon;
my sisters—Jenny, Wendy, Mary Beth;
my grandmothers—Kiki and Mere Mere;
my mother-in-law, Ellin;
my drama queen daughter, Emily—
    who provides me with a bottomless pit of material;
the Loretto Girls, Class of '73:
    Julie, Mary, Sandi, Deb, Connie, Molly, Roe,
    Janet, Debbie, Nancy, Susie, and Eileen—
    who help me put the "fun" in dysfunctional;
Carol Starr Schneider—my funny friend in LaLa Land;
and all the afflicted women I've met in my life
    who haven't lost their sense of humor.

CONTENTS

Thanks to mind-boggling advances in modern medicine, the average life expectancy for a woman in the new millennium is upward of eighty years. Think about it. *Eighty years!* That's the equivalent of:

* 10,800 tampons
* 12,587 ibuprofen tablets
* 580 haircuts
* 62 pap smears
* 80,000 fluid ounces of moisturizer

Unfortunately, many of us will spend the majority of those years suffering from water retention, cramps, breast pain, heart palpitations, irritability, sexual dysfunction, hot flashes, crippling fatigue, osteoporosis, and vaginal itch, just to name a few annoyances. Why? Because we're women. It's what we do.

Today, female complaints are out of the closet. Every newscast in America features the latest research on this disorder or that. Talk shows parade recovering addicts in front of sympathetic viewers. Celebrities are checking into Betty Ford faster than you can say "thirty days' probation." Tabloid headlines scream "Murderer Mom Blames PMS!"

Beyond the sensational headlines, there is a vast void of information. Oh sure, there are all kinds of medical guides and "wellness" books on the shelves, but none geared for hormonally challenged women like you and me—until now.

Our Syndromes, Ourselves picks up where traditional health books fall short. From PMS to Empty Nest Syndrome, menopause to midlife crisis, mainstream maladies are analyzed and interpreted in ways never heard on network TV. Newly identified conditions such as Dr. Lauranoia, Road Rag, and VADD (Vehicular Attention Deficit Disorder) are explained in nonthreatening laywoman's terms any idiot can understand. First-person case studies, written by sick women just like you, show how it's possible to live with, yes, even *celebrate,* our dysfunction in today's society!

It's a sick, sick, sick, sick, sick world and no self-respecting woman would claim to be syndrome-free. After all, what would she talk about at cocktail parties?

I wrote this book as a labor of love. If *Our Syndromes, Ourselves* can help just one woman find relief from the misery of Reunion Nervosa or Drama Queen Disorder, my efforts will have been rewarded. And if I should make enough money to pay off my bill at the pharmacy, so be it.

Thank you for buying this book. My insurance is about to run out.

CHAPTER 1

PREMENSTRUAL SYNDROME

(PMS)

THE FACTS

In 1931, while the country wallowed in the depths of the Great Depression, Dr. Robert T. Frank presented a groundbreaking paper to the New York Academy of Medicine entitled "Hormonal Causes of Premenstrual Tension." Dr. Frank had noticed the consistent appearance of certain symptoms occurring prior to menstruation, including depression, fatigue, irritability, and cravings for gefilte fish with chocolate sauce. Following Frank's presentation, gynecologists began reassuring their patients that it was common to feel "a little tense" at certain times of the month. The response from females was overwhelmingly unanimous: "Like, DUH!"

It finally took a woman, British physician Dr. Katherine Dalton, to recognize that there were dozens, if not hundreds, of *other* symptoms that occurred prior to menstruation:

* Violent mood swings
* Accident proneness
* Lowered libido
* An appetite like Orson Welles's . . .

among others. The term PMT, for "premenstrual tension," was misleading and inadequate. In 1953, Dr. Dalton published "The Premenstrual Syndrome" in the *British Medical Journal.* The article was 578,954 pages long. The condition was soon dubbed **PMS**—the grand dame of all syndromes, the drama queen of female disorders.

Today, women wear their PMS symptoms like a red badge of courage. What used to be whispered complaints between nurses or best friends have become boisterous testimonies around the water cooler. Anywhere women gather—lunch counters, break rooms, support groups—PMS is the topic of passionate and, oddly, competitive discourse:

Woman 1: "Last night, I downed a whole box of Cocoa Puffs and three wine coolers, kicked the cat through the screen door, and was in bed by nine. Let the damn kids fend for themselves."

Woman 2: "Oh, yeah? I woke up so puffy this morning, I left an imprint on the pillow like the Shroud of Turin. Then some high school kid comes to the door selling fruit for his marching band. Ever seen a tuba player run for his life? It's pathetic."

Woman 3: "That's nothing. Last week, my husband comes home late from poker night, wakes me up, and whispers, 'Hey, honey. How 'bout a little sugar!' I just lie there like I'm fast asleep but I'm plenty mad. Guy wakes up the next morning covered in Log Cabin syrup!"

Estimates of the percentage of women with premenstrual syndrome range from 40 percent to 90 percent, depending on who you talk to and what day of the month it is. Surveys indicate at least 50 percent of all women between the ages of fourteen and fifty will experience some form of PMS during any given month. Researchers know this because 50 percent of respondents wrote "Stick it up your ass!" on the "Comments" section of the surveys.

So how does a woman know if she is suffering from PMS? The Kimberly-Clark Center for PMS Awareness and Flushable Hygiene Products offers a symptoms checklist for self-diagnosis:

You may be premenstrual if . . .

1. You've just kicked the Good Humor man in the nuts
2. You're adding marshmallows to scrambled eggs
3. Your husband is suddenly agreeing with everything you say
4. Everybody around you is cowering under their desks
5. The dry cleaners have shrunk every last pair of slacks you own
6. Your breasts feel like bowling balls
7. You just doused your parish priest with pepper spray
8. The kids have gone to bed early, without being asked
9. You weep at *Love Boat* reruns
10. Your ankles are the size of five-hundred-year-old redwood trees

While there are hundreds, if not thousands, of PMS symptoms, some of the most common are:

* Unusual food cravings
* Irritability
* Aggression and violence
* Bloating and puffiness
* Weepiness

UNUSUAL FOOD CRAVINGS

To the patient with acute food cravings, PMS can be an acronym for:

Please! **M**ore **S**ugar!

or

Pour **M**ore **S**alt!

To the premenstrual woman, no taste sensation is too bizarre:

❊ Peanut butter and crawdads

❊ Caramel-dipped okra

❊ Pound cake au gratin

When premenstrual cravings for junk food are strong, they can influence a woman's buying patterns at the grocery store. In recent years, corporate America has taken notice. With sales of chocolate-covered pretzels, cookie-dough ice cream, and Reese's Pieces shooting through the roof, major manufacturers—like Hershey's, Lay's, and Ben & Jerry's—have created special divisions for "premenstrual product development." Sour Cream and Onion Pringles, Hershey's Hugs, Chunky Monkey ice cream, and Pillsbury's ready-to-spread frosting were the direct result of PMS Research and Development departments.

IRRITABILITY

During the five to seven days before the start of her period, a woman can feel cranky, disagreeable, and just plain bitchy. Due to wild fluctuations in estrogen levels, a woman's temper can ignite at the slightest provocation. During this time, doctors recommend the following tips to family and friends of the PMS patient:

* ✱ A woman with PMS is always right.
* ✱ Avoid "hot buttons" like politics, religion, and the toilet-seat debate.
* ✱ Let her have the remote control . . . just do it!
* ✱ Never say "Ah, that's just the PMS talking, honey."
* ✱ Never, *never* ask, "Didn't we just go through this three weeks ago?"

Women who spend a great deal of time together will sometimes find that their monthly cycles have synchronized. This means that an entire sorority, field hockey team, or beauty salon could, theoretically, experience premenstrual irritability at the same time.

The most striking example of this phenomenon was in 1994 when premenstrual sufferers from all fifty states marched on the nation's capital. Billed as the Billion Bitch March, it was the loudest, angriest, and hungriest mob ever to descend on the Mall in Washington, D.C. Food vendors sold record amounts of peanuts and Fudgsicles. Keynote speaker Roseanne Barr was mugged for her McDonald's french fries by a group of militant PMSers from New Haven, Connecticut. C-Span abruptly terminated their live broadcast of the rally when a riot broke out in the Porta Potti line.

AGGRESSION AND VIOLENCE

When left untreated, premenstrual irritability can escalate into acts of aggression. Some women will actually become hormonally homicidal. These PMS victims often exhibit blatant warning signs—cries for help, if you will—by wearing T-shirts that say:

I have PMS and a handgun. Any questions?

or

What's the difference between a woman with PMS and a terrorist? You can negotiate with a terrorist.

In recent years, estrogen-savvy lawyers have started using PMS as a legal defense. Accused of crimes from misdemeanors to capital offenses, female defendants are throwing themselves and their raging hormones on the mercy of the court:

Shoplifting: "I just tried the ring on, your honor, I swear! My fingers were swelling. I couldn't get the stupid thing off! I was going to return it in a few days!"

Vandalism: "If you had seen my reflection in that plate-glass window, you would have shattered it too. I only regret the rock wasn't twice as big!"

Assault and battery: "I ordered chicken enchiladas. She brought me beef!"

BLOATING AND PUFFINESS

Contributing to a woman's hostility is the problem of premenstrual water retention. For women with a propensity for salt and MSG, this symptom can be especially severe. Geri, a thirty-three-year-old market analyst, talks frankly about a bad bloating experience:

I know it was stupid. My period was due any day. But my parents were in town and they love *this little Chinese place around the corner. Well, we gorged on Kung Pao chicken, Szechuan beef, and sweet and sour pork. The next day, I'm trying to hail a cab to work. I'm wearing my purple cape and beret, trying to camouflage the pounds, you know. Suddenly, these screaming three- and four-year-olds are clamoring at my feet! They're patting my stomach and crying "Barney! Barney!" I was so mortified I took the bus. For the rest of the day, I couldn't get that damn "I love you, you love me" song out of my head!*

WEEPING SPELLS

Perhaps the most unsettling symptom of PMS is uncontrollable weeping. Without warning, the hypersensitive woman will sob incessantly over the most seemingly benign statement. This makes her extremely vulnerable to criticism, at work or at home. Friends, family, and co-workers should therefore avoid making comments to a PMS victim like:

* You look tired.
* Don't you think you're overreacting?
* You're so dramatic.
* A little grouchy today, aren't we?
* You sound just like your mother.
* What's with the attitude?
* Are you pregnant?

THE TREATMENT

The first step in controlling PMS is to anticipate your "danger days." Some gynecologists recommend that patients keep track of their symptoms in a diary or journal. Other doctors prefer that the diary be kept by a woman's partner or roommate for more objective and reliable data. The following are excerpts from the diary of Sam T., husband of Phyllis T., forty, a chronic PMS sufferer:

June 20—*Nice Phyllis.*

June 21—*Nice Phyllis.*

June 22—*Nice Phyllis.*

June 23—*Phyllis seems preoccupied and disoriented today. Searched twenty minutes for keys. Found them in ignition. Said it was my fault.*

June 24—*Phyllis annoyed with me. Something about being "underappreciated." Cried during 20/20 piece on tainted beef.*

June 26—*Phyllis inconsolable after riff at work. Something about an "office-supply conspiracy."*

June 27—*Phyllis extremely irritable today. Threatened the dog and the cable guy. Cable guy laughed it off. Spike ran away.*

June 28—*Phyllis locked herself in room after breakfast, hasn't emerged since. Kids worried. No sign of Spike.*
June 29—*Nice Phyllis!!*

Eventually, a pattern will emerge and the patient can identify the "red-flag days" of her cycle. During these days, she should take pains to avoid caffeine, salt, sugar, white flour, sharp objects, firearms, and cable repairmen.

CHAPTER 2

VEHICULAR ATTENTION DEFICIT DISORDER

VADD

THE FACTS

Ever since Henry Ford let Mrs. Ford take the Model T for a spin, men have complained about "crazy women drivers." Today, the bias against female drivers persists. That's why whenever you see a man and a woman together in a car, nine times out of ten, it's the *guy* who is driving. The subliminal message:

I am a better driver than you. My reflexes are better. My vision is better. I accelerate better. I brake better. Therefore it is I who must drive the car . . . at least until we arrive at the party. Then, I'll consume three Stolis and appoint you the designated driver because, at that point, my skills will have sunk to a level slightly below yours.

Such chauvinistic perceptions have been unfounded since, statistically, women have always had better driving records than men . . . that is, until recently. In 1999, a study by the AIPG (Association of Insurance Price Gougers) found that "soccer moms" had 20 percent more accidents than any other group of drivers. This comes as no surprise to frazzled mothers who, on any given day, must achieve NASCAR speeds attempting to cross town in the four minutes between Suzuki lessons and soccer practice. Still, the data is alarming.

Numbers don't lie. The fact is: Women are becoming more of a threat to themselves and others on the road. And while the research isn't conclusive, the cause appears to be a genetic imbalance, a condition called **Vehicular Attention Deficit Disorder,** or **VADD.**

VADD is the inability to concentrate or focus for long periods of time while operating a moving vehicle. VADD is characterized by one or more of the following symptoms:

* Inattentiveness
* Extreme distractibility
* Weak impulse control
* Difficulty following maps or directions
* Excessive car-phone use

THE SYMPTOMS

INATTENTIVENESS

Inattentiveness can take many forms. VADD victims report a sensation similar to sleepwalking, a trancelike state that occurs sporadically and unpredictably while behind the wheel. VADD causes one or more of the following behaviors:

* Running stoplights
* Sideswiping the garage
* Backing into grocery carts, bikes, or family pets
* Inability to hear sirens and other emergency vehicles
* Delayed response after the light turns green
* Driving the wrong way through the one-way pickup lane at school
* Failure to keep track of carpool days
* Losing things necessary for driving (car keys, purse with driver's license, eyeglasses)

✳ Failure to notice gas gauge is below the "E"
   or flashing warning lights

Suzi M., a busy mother of three and registered
nurse, relates her VADD experiences:

*It's this zombielike feeling. I arrive at my destination and
can't recall how I got there, the route I took, the lights I may
or may not have run, pedestrians I might have mowed down,
roadkill I may have left in my wake. I can't remember. I just
get in this zone, you know? And God help the people who
get in my way [she breaks down in tears].*

EXTREME DISTRACTIBILITY

Women afflicted with VADD can be easily distracted by just
about anything. The most common is a good-looking man.

Most women are reluctant to admit they bird-dog
members of the opposite sex because of the men-do-it-
and-men-are-pigs-therefore-I-must-be-a-pig-too stigma.
Yet the National VADD Association estimates that over
70 percent of women *will* rubberneck to watch an
attractive stud running down the street in, say, flimsy
thigh-high jogging shorts and a muscle-man T-shirt.

There are other sights that can drive a woman to
distraction from behind the wheel. Even an attractive

female strolling down the street will get a double take, especially if she is very thin or has a great haircut or snazzy shoes. Below is an incomplete list of things that can divert a VADD victim's attention:

* Hunky men
* Superthin women
* Cute kids
* Babies
* Great haircuts
* Sale signs, any size
* Cute dogs
* Garage sales
* Cute houses
* Pottery Barn
* Sam's Club

Andrea W., a thirty-something CPA, recounts:

I was on my way to the dentist when, out of the corner of my eye, I noticed a close-out sale sign in the window of Pier 1 way over on the frontage road. Without considering my safety or the safety of others, I swerved over three whole lanes to make my exit, forcing a bus full of Baptist convention-goers into a ditch. I stopped just long enough to see that they were okay, then sped off to the sale. I'm so embarrassed now. So ashamed.

I've since made amends to the people I hurt. No amount of tiki torches are worth risking human life, not even at 50 percent off.

WEAK IMPULSE CONTROL

A woman afflicted with VADD will have difficulty controlling simple impulses. The most common manifestation of this symptom is another syndrome, Cosmetic Compulsive Disorder, or CCD. CCD is the irresistible urge to touch up your makeup, comb your hair, even change your clothes while driving. Women at risk for CCD will answer "yes" to one or more of the following questions:

* Do you frequently adjust your rearview mirror to see yourself, rather than the traffic in back of you?
* Are there more cosmetics in the console of your car than in your bathroom at home?
* Has a sudden stop ever caused you to apply lipstick to your neck?

Women afflicted with CCD are often in denial and therefore untreatable by most traditional methods of therapy. Rationalization is a common trait in these patients, who believe they present no danger to the driving public at large.

Sylvie T., a twenty-nine-year-old Chicagoland commuter writes:

I drive an hour to work in the city five days a week. I'd rather sleep that extra hour than spend it in the bathroom every morning. Sure, it's probably a bit dangerous, but I'm in complete control. I am proud to say I can pluck my eyebrows, put on an entire face, curl my hair, change shoes, and shave my legs, if need be . . . my eyes never leaving the JFK Expressway. Once, after an especially bad coffee spill, I changed my jacket and my blouse while traveling at sixty miles per hour. VADD? Humbug! This is a life skill, not a disorder!

Other women find CCD to be a real concern and will typically seek treatment in twelve-step programs or thirty-day inpatient clinics. Sally, thirty-two, a paralegal from Orange County, California, who currently attends MMA (Mobile Makeovers Anonymous) meetings twice a week, recounts the day she "hit bottom":

I had to deliver a brief in L.A. County one morning and I was running late. I remember thinking: No biggie. I'll just put on my mascara in the car on the way. I sped off to the freeway on-ramp and settled into the middle lane, which I thought would take me all the way into downtown without a lot of lane changes. The traffic was heavy but manageable. Feeling a little cocky, I fished the mascara out of my purse and took off my glasses for a quick touch-up. The next thing I remember is the sound of screeching brakes and my tube of Great Lash falling to the floor. The surgeon was able to save the eye but my peripheral vision is pretty much shot.

DIFFICULTY FOLLOWING MAPS OR DIRECTIONS

Women with VADD may develop a type of "directional dyslexia." Geographic terms like north, south, east, and west mean nothing. Mile markers and odometers are useless. Many victims learn to compensate by teaching friends and family to accommodate their disability by adapting directions to a language they can understand.

Below is an example of how an acquaintance of Marian O. (a VADD sufferer from Kent, Indiana) adapted directions to a furniture store. These simple changes allowed Marian to drive independently to a sofa sale, thereby increasing her self-esteem while enhancing the look of her family room:

BEFORE: *East 1.5 miles to Oak St., south on Oak three blocks to Maple, east on Maple 3.8 miles to I-44. South on I-44 nine miles to Highland exit, west 2.2 miles on Highland to Miller Furniture (north side of street).*

AFTER: *Go a smidge past Food Mart, turn right (toward Bev's house). Go past the park where we used to make out in high school. Turn on the street with the tacky pink house on the corner. Drive about ten or fifteen minutes to that highway everybody takes to the Christmas-tree farm. Stay on it till you see the old Stuckey's. Turn off. Go left and drive for a while till you see the antique mall where Connie bought her daybed. Turn in next to the Adirondack chairs.*

EXCESSIVE CAR-PHONE USE

The proliferation of cell phones has exacerbated the problems of VADD sufferers tenfold. Many afflicted women find it impossible to refrain from chatting on the phone while barreling through stop signs, cruising for garage sales, and maneuvering through carpool lanes. By itself, car phone use is not a hazardous activity. But it becomes potentially lethal when combined with the following VADD behaviors:

* ✳ Applying lipstick, mascara, or blush
* ✳ Changing panty hose
* ✳ Reading directions
* ✳ Eating a Big Mac and fries
* ✳ Fishing for pacifiers on the floor

THE TREATMENT

As awareness of VADD increases, the medical community and the Department of Motor Vehicles work tirelessly to find a cure for this dangerous disease. A vaccine is expected by the year 2004.

In the meantime, the best defense against the disease is prevention. Experts recommend the use of special audiocassettes to keep VADD in check. Designed to be used in the car every time a woman takes the wheel, the tapes ask the driver to repeat calming affirmations like:

* *I'm keeping my eyes on the road.*
* *I'm watching my rearview mirror.*
* *I know exactly where I'm going.*
* *I'm checking my blind spot.*
* *I am in control.*
* *That Target store doesn't interest me in the least.*

Used religiously, the tapes have been proven to reduce accidents and other vehicular mishaps by up to 60 percent . . . except in densely populated areas near outlet malls.

CHAPTER 3

MENOPAUSE AND PERIMENOPAUSE SYDROME

MAPS

THE FACTS

From the moment a baby girl is born, her body begins a morphing process not unlike the Incredible Hulk on a bad day. The baby fat of childhood turns into the bony knees and concave chest of pre-adolescence. Then, breasts start to bud and hips appear where there were none. The onset of menses causes five- to ten-pound weight fluctuations on a monthly basis. Later, pregnancy. Periods stop but her belly swells to the size of a Best of Show watermelon at the county fair. Breast-feeding subjects the mammary glands to a daily tug-of-war. The body shrinks back to normal size (if she's lucky), only to inflate again with each subsequent pregnancy. Come the late thirties, early forties and her hair turns gray, eyes start to go, hips spread, breasts sag. Then and only then can she enjoy what doctors ironically call "the change of life," or **menopause**.

Menopause is a natural event whereby a woman's estrogen levels naturally begin to plummet and the body reacts by naturally running amok. In the past, post-menopausal women were considered "dried up," "over the hill," or "old prunes." That's why older women never actually utter words like "menopause," "the change," or "female complaints" aloud. They tap them out in Morse code.

In recent years, women's organizations like NOW (National Organization for Women) and LATOR (Losing All Tabs on Reality) have tried to put a positive spin on menopause by focusing on the "upside" of "the change":

* No more pregnancy worries
* No more monthly periods
* Need for less sleep
* Feeling more "in the moment"
* Flashes of deep insight

✳   Acquired "wisdom" and "grace"
✳   The ability to grow hair in places you never dreamed of

But no matter how hard they tried to put a smiley face on it, most women still think of menopause as one giant pain in the estrogen-deprived patootie. Why? Because unlike other syndromes, the list of symptoms associated with menopause would run off this page and onto your carpet. Here are seven of the most common symptoms, listed in order from "most annoying" to "unbearably gross":

✳   Hot flashes
✳   Mood swings
✳   Memory lapses, or brain fog
✳   The "disappearing waistline"
✳   Incontinence
✳   Changes in libido
✳   Burning tongue

THE SYMPTOMS

HOT FLASHES

Imagine a rush of intense heat to the head and neck, causing blood cells under the skin to dilate until you look like

Ed McMahon. This is a hot flash or, as some suspiciously upbeat menopausers call it, "power surge." Lasting anywhere from a few seconds to the length of a time-share presentation, a flash can cause a woman to flush in the face, perspire profusely, and rip off her clothes faster than Demi Moore.

The most troublesome type of hot flash is a phenomenon called "night sweats." This occurs while a woman is sleeping soundly, happily dreaming of having sex with Sean Connery. The torrent of heat causes her to awake, breathing rapidly and sweating like a horse, kick off her covers, and strip to her birthday suit. Staggeringly, some men misinterpret these symptoms as a come-on. Nothing could be further from the truth.

MOOD SWINGS

As estrogen levels ebb and flow, so does the menopausal woman's disposition. One minute, she's making dinner singing a Disney tune. The next, she's taking a saw to Dad's favorite chair. Mood swings can be confusing for a woman's family and friends, who never know who they're dealing with from one minute to the next:

* Mother Teresa or Mommie Dearest?
* Princess Grace or Grace Jones?
* The Good Witch of the North or the Wicked Witch of the West?

✳ The Madonna or Madonna?
✳ June Cleaver or Madwoman with a Meat
   Cleaver?

MEMORY LAPSES

Periodic short-term memory loss is a big clue that
menopause may be upon you. This so-called "menofog"
or "brain flatulence" can be particularly disturbing, especially when a woman realizes she is standing, say, in the
middle of a gas station in her nightie. Sometimes, it's hard
to discern whether these "senior moments" are due to
menopause or the everyday preoccupations of life. The
following quiz will help you determine if you are experiencing menofog:

1. Your husband wants to use your car to run an errand
   and he needs your keys. What do you do?
      A. Fumble around in your purse until he says,
         "Forget it. I'll use the spares."
      B. Go to the toilet, because that's where you
         found them last time.
      C. Can't remember the question.
2. You order a Value Meal #3 at the drive-through
   window of the local McDonald's. Do you . . .
      A. Drive off without getting your change?

      B. Drive off without getting your food?

      C. Have any idea what the question is?

3. It is Wednesday morning at ten o'clock. Are you ...

      A. Missing a doctor's appointment?

      B. Missing a dental appointment?

      C. Asking yourself, "Why am I reading this book? I'm two hours late for work!"

4. You often lose your glasses and find them ...

      A. On your head.

      B. On your nose.

      C. On somebody's else nose.

If you answered A, B, or C to any or all of these questions, you've probably forgotten everything you've read up to this point and won't remember anything from here on, so ... never mind.

THE DISAPPEARING WAISTLINE

Women tend to store their body fat in three distinct ways:

1. The "apple" shape (weight distributed around the middle)
2. The "pear" shape (weight distributed around the hips)
3. The "cantaloupe" shape (weight distributed all over, causing the body to form a perfect sphere)

During menopause, the distribution of fat often shifts, causing "pears" to become "apples" and, sometimes, "apples" to become "cantaloupes." This is called the "disappearing waistline" syndrome.

The disappearing waistline is due to an alteration of the WHR, or Waist-Hip Ratio. WHR refers to the relationship between your hip measurement and your waist measurement. You can calculate your own WHR by using the following formula:

* Measure your waist and divide by half (just to make yourself feel better).
* Measure your hips and divide by half (that's what I always do).
* Subtract your waist measurement from your hip measurement.
* Multiply the difference by two to get your WHR number.
* If the number is 8 or higher, you are a "pear."
* If the number is lower than 8, you are an "apple."

WARNING: If you have a negative number, you are an overripe, juicy cantaloupe. If you're not menopausal, you're awfully damn close.

INCONTINENCE

The loss of bladder control can be embarrassing, incon-venient, and downright frightening. Some women live in constant fear of sneezing, coughing, *I Love Lucy* reruns . . . anything that might cause a leak in the dam. It's depressing, especially to the woman who—throughout her adult life—has always required running water, ocean sounds, and thirty minutes of uninterrupted throne time just to leave a urine sample at the doctor's office. For these women, the irony is simply too much to bear.

CHANGES IN LIBIDO

Women in the throes of menopause tend to run hot and cold when it comes to sex. On the one hand, the freedom from pregnancy worries allows a woman to "act on the moment." On the other hand, dropping estrogen levels can reduce her desire so that, as one husband put it, "I check my libido at the door." The following is a hypothetical conver-sation that might transpire between a menopausal woman and her partner on the way home from a romantic movie.

WOMAN: Mmm, that love scene in the elevator was so *hot*. I think, I think I'm in the mood, Stanley.

MAN: Mmmm, me too, baby. I'll hurry home.

WOMAN: No, I mean I think I'm in the mood now. Take me. Take me *now,* Stanley.

MAN: Right now?

WOMAN: Mmm, yes! Yes, right now, Stanley. Pull over. Pull over and let's play elevator operator!

MAN: Uh, okay. *(Pulling over to the curb.)*

WOMAN: FOR GOD'S SAKE, NOT HERE, STANLEY! YOU THINK I WANT EVERYBODY AND THEIR PIG WATCHING?

MAN: But you said "now" . . .

WOMAN: WHY MUST YOU ALWAYS TAKE ME LITERALLY, STANLEY! YOU'D LOVE THAT, WOULDN'T YOU? HAVING YOUR WAY WITH ME WHILE ALL THE NEIGHBORS WERE WATCHING? THAT'D MAKE STANLEY A BIG MAN AROUND TOWN, WOULDN'T IT?!!

MAN: But honey . . .

WOMAN: DON'T *HONEY* ME . . .
           (She bursts into tears.)
           Let's just snuggle a bit, okay? I love it when
           we snuggle 'cuz you're my wittle huggy bear.
           Does my wittle huggy bear want some
           honey? Hmmm?

MAN: Well, if you're sure.

WOMAN: Mmmmm, I wuv my wittle huggy bear so
           much . . . let me show how much . . .

MAN: Ooh, baby.

WOMAN: *(Sitting up.)* By the way, the insurance company
           called and said they want a second estimate
           on the car before they settle. CAN YOU
           BELIEVE THAT? AS IF I HAVE THE
           TIME TO DRIVE AROUND TOWN
           VISITING BODY SHOPS! YOU BETTER
           GIVE THEM A CALL TOMORROW
           AND GIVE THEM HELL. THEY'LL
           LISTEN TO YOU. YOU'RE A MAN.
           IS IT HOT IN HERE?

BURNING TONGUE

As if the above symptoms aren't bad enough, menopause can cause your tongue to actually catch fire. Experts attribute this bizarre disorder to hormonal changes in the mouthal environment, causing a depletion of saliva essential for swallowing, spitting, and whistling "Dixie." Of course, burning tongue syndrome is very rare, but it's something to be aware of . . . particularly if you live close to a gas station or drink your vodka straight.

Although women in midlife have been painfully aware of "the change" for generations, there's a relatively new syndrome on the scene causing younger women to quake in their boots—**perimenopause,** or "Change of Life: The Prequel." Perimenopause simply means you don't have to wait until you're forty-five, fifty, or fifty-five years of age to enjoy the aforementioned symptoms. You can have it all in your late thirties and early forties! And that's just peri, peri peachy, ain't it?

THE TREATMENT

The medical establishment recommends Hormone Replacement Therapy, or HRT, for the treatment of menopausal symptoms. In fact, many women seem to find relief by combining supplemental estrogen with the occasional glass of wine, tequila shot, or Prozac. Feel free to experiment to find the right combination for you.

CHAPTER 4

DOES MY BUTT LOOK BIG? SYNDROME

(DMBLBS)

THE FACTS

In the late 1800s, the hottest thing on the runways of Paris and New York was the bustle, that pointless but oddly striking wad of fabric attached to the backside of a skirt. The bustle hid a multitude of sins and provided needed padding for women forced to ride on hard, bumpy buggy benches without so much as a rubber baby buggy bumper to absorb the shock. But like all things trendy, the bustle eventually went the way of the chamber pot, leaving women to deal with the harsh reality of their backsides.

Today, American women try anything and everything to achieve the shrinkage—if not total elimination—of their bottoms. Herbal wraps, massage, steam baths, rubber suits, vibrating belts, and elective surgery—all have been employed in an effort to make perfectly good derrieres disappear. Since only two women in history have actually succeeded in making their rears vanish completely (Twiggy and Calista Flockhart), the remaining female population has become obsessed by the width, breadth, and girth of their heinies. This preoccupation is called **Does My Butt Look Big? Syndrome,** or **DMBLBS.**

As syndromes go, DMBLBS is unique in that it will touch virtually every woman in the world at some point in her life. Fat or thin, big-boned or small, pear-shaped or apple, DMBLBS doesn't discriminate. This is what makes it such an insidious and devastating disorder. Although women with DMBLBS will display a variety of symptoms, the most common are:

* Fanny-pack phobia
* Compulsive buttock clenching
* Inappropriate butt comparisons
* Fixation with mirrors and plate-glass windows
* A preoccupation with Lycra

THE SYMPTOMS

FANNY-PACK PHOBIA

Women afflicted with DMBLBS will typically exhibit an extreme and irrational fear of fanny packs. Introduced in the mid-'80s as a utilitarian alternative to the handbag, the fanny pack allowed women to cart their vital necessities— car keys, lipstick, tampons, Mace, Sam's Club card—in a small nylon pouch attached to a strap that was worn around the waist. Fanny packs could have been the greatest fashion accessory ever invented had it not been for one irrefutable fact: They make your butt look bigger than Elsie the Cow's. Rachel S., thirty-one, from New Jersey, is a former fanny-pack devotee who was shocked into reality during an incident at an amusement park:

I bought my first fanny pack in 1984 and wore it to this hot new amusement park, Six Flags over Sweaty, Stinky People. For the first time in my adult life, I could ride a roller coaster without worrying if my purse was going to spill Tampax everywhere. It was great! Then, as I was wandering through the House of Nausea, I caught a glimpse of the biggest butt I'd ever seen in my life in one of the mirrors. That butt was mine! At first, I thought it was one of those wavy trick mirrors. Then I realized— I was in the ladies room! This was no trick. This was a fanny-

pack freak show!! I ran out of the rest room and flung the pack into the Log Ride Thru Suspiciously Blue Water (after removing my Sam's Club card, of course). To this day, I can't smell funnel cakes or a Coney dog without having a fanny-pack flashback!

COMPULSIVE BUTTOCK CLENCHING

DMBLB Syndrome causes certain behaviors that are decidedly bizarre. One of the most curious is the intentional compression of the buttocks. Just as a woman will hold in her stomach muscles when she's being measured for a new dress, the DMBLBS sufferer will suck in her "butt cheeks" to give the illusion of a tighter backside. The most advanced cheek clenchers can reduce their hip measurements by up to three inches. Unfortunately, this is a subtle and delicate technique that can take years to perfect. Without proper training, rookies attempting butt compressions can throw out a disk or dislocate the pelvis.

INAPPROPRIATE BUTT COMPARISONS

Victims of DMBLBS are fraught with insecurities. Exacerbating the problem is their inexhaustible fascination with how their butt compares to every other woman's butt in the universe. As an example of this, here is a transcript from a group-therapy session recorded at the Women's Center for Holistic Buttock Acceptance in Palo Alto, California. These patients had been admitted to the center's thirty-day rehabilitation program, called "Loving Your Buttocks Fully." The names have been changed to protect their identities:

BETTY: Uh, yeah. My name is Betty and . . . does my butt look big in this hospital gown?

THERAPIST: Betty, we're not here to talk about our buttocks right now. Just tell us a little bit about yourself.

BETTY: Well, I'm from Portland, where I work as an office manager. It's a medical office with about twelve women, seven of whom have bigger butts than me. It used to be six, but Darla Cummings put on a lot of weight after she sprained her ankle—

THERAPIST: Okay, moving on. Next?

CAROL: I'm Carol. I'm from San Diego and I can really relate to Betty. I feel so close to her right now . . . *(getting choked up)* and . . . and

I just want to say . . . *(Pauses)* . . . Doctor, whose butt is bigger—mine or Betty's?

THERAPIST: Now, Carol. In order to heal, we have to stop comparing our bodies with others. *Own* your buttocks. It's okay. But let Betty own her *own* buttocks, too! That's the way to holistic buttock acceptance.

MARJORIE: I'm Marjorie. And that was so beautiful. *(Sighs.)* I'm from Kansas City, where there are lots of big butts. It's the barbecue. But I know, deep in my heart, that the size of your butt doesn't matter. It's what you do with it that counts. Oops. Or is that something else? Anyway, I'm ready to make friends with my butt . . . as long as I know it's not as big as Betty's.

FIXATION WITH MIRRORS AND PLATE-GLASS WINDOWS

When a woman is afflicted with DMBLBS, she will develop a peculiar love-hate fixation with mirrors and other reflective objects, like plate-glass windows. On one hand, the woman *needs* the mirror to assess the exact proportions of her butt at any given moment in time.

Ironically, it's that same mirror that causes her the most pain, particularly when the reflection reveals a butt bigger than the ideal butt she desires.

To cope with the pain, sufferers often employ a defense mechanism known as "big butt transference." This is when the woman projects her anxieties about her butt to the mirror and will blame the reflection in the glass for distorting reality: *It's not my butt, it's a fat mirror!* "Big butt transference" can be dangerous, as it will cause women to purchase expensive slacks with a false sense of security, only to find that their butts look bigger than ever when they get home from the store.

PREOCCUPATION WITH LYCRA

Women with DMBLBS are constantly searching for new ways to tighten their tushies. On any given day, lingerie departments are full of DMBLBS sufferers sampling and testing the latest foundations. These ladies collect Lycra like Madonna collects men. Many of them use a secret code to rate girdles, body briefers, control-top panties, and compression shorts by three criteria:

1. Holding power
2. Price
3. Estimated time before circulation in the legs is cut off completely

Lycraphiles will share this information via support groups, newsletters, and Web sites. Some have even formed buying clubs to take advantage of high-volume discounts.

THE TREATMENT

To date, the most effective method of treatment for DMBLBS is aversion therapy, or "counterconditioning." In a controlled and safe environment, the patient is subjected to a "sensory overload" of buttock-related stimuli for forty-eight hours straight:

* Coppertone ads
* *NYPD Blue* episodes
* Eddie Murphy monologues
* The campfire scene from *Blazing Saddles*
* Tasteless fart jokes
* Sumo wrestling matches

In most cases, the patient will "break" somewhere around the forty-second hour and profess her desire never to look at another butt again, including her own.

CHAPTER 5

IDENTITY CRISIS

(IC)

THE FACTS

Those biblical women had it made. With only one name to worry about—Ruth, Mary, Rebekah, Esther—they saved a fortune on monogrammed towels and stone tablets. Unfortunately, as more people populated the Earth, villages became crowded with mulitple Ruths and Marys, forcing the IRS to look for ways to discern one woman from the next. For a while, the best they could come up with was something like:

✽ Mary from Nazareth, Wife of Joseph
✽ Rebekah from the House of Isaac

✳ Bambi, King Herod's Gal Friday and Personal Masseuse

Soon society adopted the use of surnames, the patri-archal system that assigns a woman the last name of her father and, later, her husband. For centuries, people thought this seemed to work pretty well, except in rare cases when a woman's first name just didn't fit with her husband's last name, such as:

✳ Kelly Kelley

✳ Ura Schmuck

✳ Ima Ho

Then, in the 1960s, some radical-thinking women started asking themselves:

✳ *Who am I?*

✳ *What's in a name?*

✳ *Why am I wearing this hideous fringed vest?*

They decided to rebel against the status quo. Some brides decided to retain their maiden names. Others chose to hyphenate their last names to their husband's. Some couples even *combined* last names, resulting in a melting pot of new appellations, such as McFinklestein, Steinvaggen, and Johnsonbogdonovich.

Today, a 57 percent divorce rate combined with a second generation of cross-hyphenating offspring have caused females at the millennium to ask:

❊ *What's my name again?*

These women are having what is called an **Identity Crisis.**

An Identity Crisis is a blanket term for any condition or event that causes a woman to question who she really is. The crisis can manifest itself in many ways and at any age. It can occur only once in a lifetime or—in the case of celebrities—on a daily basis. The most common manifestations of an Identity Crisis are:

❊ What's My Name Crisis
❊ Bad Hair Day Crisis
❊ Disassociative Wardrobe Personality Disorder
❊ The Madonna/Whore Underwear Syndrome

THE SYMPTOMS

WHAT'S MY NAME CRISIS

As described on the previous page, this crisis occurs when a woman is in transition due to marriage, divorce, or remarriage and must change her name accordingly. Lately, cultural anthropologists have observed new cases of complex cross-hyphenation in which a hyphenated female marries a hyphenated male. The wedding invitation always reads something like this:

> *Mr. Robert Fortenberry, Jr., and Mrs. Alecia*
> *Goldsmith-Fortenberry*
> *request the honor of your presence at*
> *the marriage of their daughter*
> *Miss Melissa Marie Goldsmith-Fortenberry*
> *to*
> *Mr. Jonathan Blaine Sunderby-Wallingford*
> *son of*
> *Mr. Blaine Thaddeus Wallingford and Mrs. Margaret*
> *Sunderby-Wallingford*

After the ceremony, what will the bride be called?

A. Melissa Goldsmith-Fortenberry-Sunderby-Wallingford
B. Mrs. Jonathan Blaine Sunderby-Wallingford
C. Missy Goldenberry-Sunderford
D. Hey, you!

More importantly, what will their *children* be called and will there be enough room on the birth certificate?

Truly a modern dilemma, this crisis has led to the renewed popularity of single names, such as Cher, Roseanne, Brandy, and Madonna.

THE BAD HAIR DAY CRISIS

Some experts, 100 percent of whom are male, pooh-pooh the notion that a woman's entire personality can be altered simply by a bad hair day. To these experts, women answer: "Pooh-pooh on you."

A recent scientific study, conducted by the National Institute for Follicular Affairs in fifty Target stores across the country, concluded that a bad hair day is the single most common "trigger" of an identity crisis.

To comprehend the magnitude of the problem, consider the investment a woman makes in her hair. Statistics show the average woman uses twelve to seventeen hair products every day, including shampoo, conditioner, hot-oil treatment, styling gel, scalp revitalizer, mousse, spritz, sparkle gel, hair spray, brush, comb, ponytail holders, barrettes, headbands, clippies, scrunchies, extensions, falls, and bobby pins. With a regular cut, color, and perm, a woman can spend upward of $9,000 per month on her hair. Is it any wonder that a bad hair day can have devastating, disruptive consequences?

Complicating matters is society's attitude that "hair makes the woman." Indeed, you *can* tell a lot about a woman by her hairstyle :

$$\begin{array}{rcl}
\text{Big hair} & = & \text{Country singer} \\
\text{Huge hair} & = & \text{TV evangelist} \\
\text{Chin-length bob} & = & \text{TV anchor} \\
\text{"Wedge" cut} & = & \text{The entire LPGA tour}
\end{array}$$

But when a bad hair day occurs, a woman loses all perspective and forgets, albeit just until the next shampoo, what she's all about. Could Dolly Parton sing a note if she had flat hair? Would Hillary Clinton dream of campaigning in hair extensions? Of course not. When a woman's hair isn't right, she just doesn't feel like herself. Ask Jane Pauley.

DISSOCIATIVE WARDROBE PERSONALITY DISORDER

It is a known fact that eight out of ten women are susceptible to a rare condition, not unlike multiple personality disorder, that strikes every time we go shopping for clothes. That's why, in every woman's closet, you'll find three distinct wardrobes:

❋ The practical wardrobe

❋ The trendy wardrobe

❋ The "what the hell was I thinking?" wardrobe

Dissociative Wardrobe Personality Disorder is a common form of the Identity Crisis. One day, a woman will take a meeting in a tailored navy-blue suit from Ann Taylor. The next, she's conducting a conference in a leotard, sarong, and platform sandals. While scientists have no definitive explanation for this extreme style vacillation, there is an accepted theory: It's what's on sale, stupid!

Dissociative Wardrobe Personality Disorder is usually caused by a clothes-related trauma in early childhood. Terri, a forty-two-year-old stockbroker from Westport, Connecticut, tells her story:

I attended parochial school, where we were required to wear gray wool jumpers every day of the week. There was a very strict dress code. The nuns had rules for everything, except shoes. One day in sixth grade, Kathleen Ann O'Shaunnessey had the nerve to come to school wearing go-go boots just like the ones the dancers wore on Shindig. *We were all blown away. Well, Sister Mary Chastity took one look at Kathleen's feet, grabbed her by the ponytail, and dragged her down to Mother Superior's office. What a commotion! Screaming, crying, then the horrifying sound of relentless hammering. I've never been so afraid. As we left school that day, we passed the large crucifix outside the chapel. There, nailed to Jesus' feet, were Kathleen's go-go boots. I decided right then and there that no one would dictate fashion to Theresa Marie Wilfington! I got expelled that year for excessive dress-code violations. But I offered it up to Kathleen Ann.*

THE MADONNA/WHORE UNDERWEAR SYNDROME

Somewhere around age thirty, or immediately following the birth of her first child, a woman develops an inexplicable attraction to cotton, old-lady underwear. Her need for comfort suddenly overrides the desire for the skimpy, lacy lingerie of her youth. This causes a serious inner conflict called the Madonna/Whore Underwear Syndrome.

On the one hand, a woman wants desperately to feel sexy in that flimsy black thong from Victoria's Secret. On the other hand, she's sick and tired of ducking around corners to pick fabric out of her crack. This dichotomy forces many women to lead double lives. Wilma A., a thirty-two-year-old paralegal from Tulsa, Oklahoma, describes her daily struggle with Madonna/Whore:

For the past eight years, my husband has given me the same gift for birthdays, Christmas, Valentine's Day, and anniversaries—matching bra and panties. I've got 'em in leopard, tiger, cheetah, and Holstein. Red lace, black lace, paisley,

and polka dot. I've got push-ups, peek-a-boos, padded, and
unpadded. Backless, cupless, and crotchless. I have an entire
dresser full of the stuff. Every morning, I wait until my hus-
band leaves the house before I get dressed. Then I sneak down
to my secret "tidy whities" stash in the basement. I put on
plain white underpants, a cotton Playtex bra, and leave for
work with the fancy underwear in my purse, just in case. My
worst nightmare is getting in a terrible car accident and hear-
ing the surgeon tell my husband, "She's in postop. You can
claim your wife's personal effects and those old-lady underpants
at the nurses' station."

THE TREATMENT

While psychologists continue to search for ways to help
the woman in Identity Crisis, a promising course of treatment has emerged from the Three Faces of Eve Institute
in Tucson, Arizona. There, a pioneering psychiatrist named
the Doctor Formerly Known as Vince has developed a
radical program based on ancient Indian healing rituals.

On the first of the patient's ten-day stay at the institute,
she is driven deep into the desert, naked, with only a mirror, a case of granola bars, and one *People* magazine in her
backpack. The idea is for the patient to experience the

"oneness of her inner and outer selves" as her dominant personality kills off the auxiliary personalities who dare to try to cop her food and the "Best and Worst Dressed Celebrities" issue. Nine out of ten patients come forth from the desert fully integrated and, essentially, cured.

CHAPTER 6

PREMARITAL STRESS SYNDROME

PMSS

THE FACTS

Thanks to feminist foot soldiers like Betty Friedan, Gloria Steinem, and Doctor Barbie, society has changed its attitude about single women. A woman no longer needs a wedding ring to feel complete. Today's w-o-m-a-n can bring home the bacon, fry it up in the pan, and crumble it on a Cobb salad just in time for *Ally McBeal*. She can venture virtually anywhere without an escort—movies, restaurants, Mount Everest, even the sperm bank.

Today's woman has more to do with her time than worry about finding a husband. She's got a career, credit card debt, Oprah's Book Club, the gym, and the Psychic Friends Network. Her marital status is a nonissue . . . except, of course, to her mother, sisters, and every married aunt, cousin, and girlfriend within meddling distance.

A single woman over the age of twenty-five is under enormous pressure to find Mr. Right and *find him NOW.* This pressure, applied often and relentlessly by "well-intentioned" loved ones, creates a crippling condition known as **Premarital Stress Syndrome,** or **PMSS.**

PMSS strikes approximately 40 percent of single women over twenty-five, 60 percent of women over thirty, and an alarming 80 percent of women thirty-five and over. (For unmarried females over forty, the numbers are off the charts.) In response to these dramatic statistics, PMSS support groups have popped up all over the country. The National Association for the Advancement of Single People (NAASP) has made great strides in bringing this serious but often ignored syndrome into the national consciousness.

Premarital Stress Syndrome causes a variety of mini-disorders that can adversely affect a single woman's mental health. The most common are:

✳ Fix-up Phobia

✳ Singles Barfluenza

✳ Personal Adverticulitus
✳ Always a Bridesmaid Syndrome

FIX-UP PHOBIA

One of the most common subsyndromes of PMSS is the paralyzing fear of blind dates with a "friend of a friend," sometimes called "Fix-up Phobia." According to the National Blind-Date Tracking Center in Cape Canaveral, Florida, ninety-three out of one hundred fix-ups end in disaster. Experts attribute these discouraging statistics to the following factors:

1. Unrealistic expectations (he's expecting Pamela Anderson; she expects something more than a Whopper with fries).

2. False pretenses (he assumes her breasts are real; she figures his toupee is a joke to break the ice).

3. Nothing in common (she likes "long walks on the beach, fine wine, and Nat King Cole"; he's into "long naps on the La-Z-Boy, cheap beer, and Weird Al Yankovic").

SINGLES BARFLUENZA

Occasionally, in spite of her better judgment, a woman with acute PMSS will succumb to peer pressure and enter the dark and surreal world that is the singles bar. Her rationale: *Maybe this time I'll find a guy who wants to talk to my face and not my boobs.* This type of detached-from-reality thinking is typical of PMSS victims. A healthy person would realize how ridiculous this impossible dream truly is.

When a woman with PMSS walks into a singles-bar environment, she becomes susceptible to a highly contagious condition known as barfluenza. Sometimes referred to as the "rockin' pneumonia" or the "boogie-woogie flu," barfluenza is believed to have originated in New York's Studio 54 in January of '71. *The only known carriers of the virus are men.* Early warning signs include:

   ❋   Disco fever

   ❋   Painfully lame pickup lines

   ❋   Roving hands

   ❋   High rejection-recovery rate

Women should take every precaution to avoid carriers of barfluenza. Sometimes, however, it's too late to prevent exposure to the grisly disease. Emma K., a twenty-eight-year-old advertising executive, remembers her first barfluenza infection:

It was kinda dark and smoky but the guy seemed good-look-ing and almost charming. And, except for the Aqua Velva, he was sending out all the right vibes. The longer we talked, the more I drank. And the more I drank, the more attractive he became. Soon, I was inviting him over to my place. The next morning, I woke up to the most nauseating sight I've ever seen in bed next to me. Think Walter Matthau in Dirty Old Men. *I found out later I was a victim of what gay men call the "cosmetic effect of darkness," a common symptom of barfluenza. From now on, the only bars I'm going into are juice bars . . . and in broad daylight!*

PERSONAL ADVERTICULITUS

When premarital pressure becomes too intense, some women are forced to take drastic and sometimes danger-ous measures. The most risky of these are personal ads. For the uninitiated, the experience can be as frightening as *The Blair Witch Project* on a full stomach.

First, the woman must learn the complicated and confusing universal code of singles ads:

SWF—Single White Female

SBCM—Single Black Christian Male

GHAN/SMNK—Gay Hispanic Asian Nonsmoking Male No Kids

AWBiMDNS3K÷2—Alcoholic White Bisexual Doctor Nonsmoker Three Kids Shared Custody

Once a woman has deciphered the code, she must screen hundreds of ads for a possible match. This can be a confusing task, since personal ads are not always what they seem. In fact, false advertising has become such a problem that the NAASP has recently published a booklet entitled *Singles Ads for Dummies—What They* Really *Mean*. Below are examples of actual singles ads, translated to their true meaning by specially trained linguists:

Actual Personal Ad	*Translation*
INTELLECTUAL INSATIABLE SWM, 27, educated in New England and cultured in Europe, seeks well-built woman for friendship and more. Yes, I do have a body and face to go with my charm.	GULLIBLE GIRLS ONLY 27-year-old single white male, graduated in top 75% of his class at Dover (Delaware) High, backpacked in Amsterdam for legal pot. 95-lb. weakling with acne.
RELATIONSHIP ORIENTED DBM, 35, 5'10", 185 lbs, seeks a S/DF, looks not important. I'm slightly effeminate and tattooed. I like cycling, travel, sappy movies, tact, and wit. Single mothers welcome to respond.	NEED HELP WITH THE RENT Divorced black male, pushing 40, maybe 5'8", 200-plus pounds, will take anybody at this point. I'm trying to convince myself and my parents I'm not gay.

DREAM WEAVER
SWM, 41, 6', follicularly challenged, honest, never married, no excess baggage, too
busy for mating rituals,
seeking lovely lady who isn't
afraid to try new things.

STUCK IN THE '70S
41-year-old, single white
bald guy, loser with no life,
afraid of approaching a
woman face-to-face, seeks
female for experimental
hair grafting.

ALWAYS A BRIDESMAID SYNDROME

One of the most debilitating afflictions suffered by
women with PMSS is a type of post-traumatic disorder
called Always a Bridesmaid Syndrome, or ABS. ABS
occurs in unmarried women between the ages of twenty-
two and thirty-four who have served as bridesmaids in
more weddings than they can count. Over 64 percent of
these women will exhibit the following symptoms:

* A growing collection of ghastly dresses and dyed-
  to-match shoes in peach, lavender, emerald
  green, and thirteen shades of pink
* A violent aversion to taffeta
* Fear of flying bouquets
* Auditory disorders, including ringing in the ears
  to the tune of "Here Comes the Bride" and
  "We've Only Just Begun"

Compounding her problem, the ABS victim often feels obliged to entertain single male members of the wedding party at the reception. This can lead to tragic dance-floor encounters involving inebriated, oversexed twenty-year-olds who propose marriage after the first slow dance.

THE TREATMENT

Of course, the only surefire cure for Premarital Stress Syndrome is marriage. Most women are not willing to go to such extremes until they're sure they've suffered enough.

The next best treatment is a classic ruse perfected by Elwood P. Dowd in *Harvey* and Jan Brady—the imaginary friend or, in this case, imaginary fiancé.

CHAPTER 7

MIDLIFE CRISIS

THE FACTS

At some point between her fortieth and fiftieth birthday, a woman will experience what mental-health professionals call a "defining midlife moment":

* Discovering your first gray hair
* Attending the marriage of your college roommate's son
* Tweezing your first chin whisker
* Buying your first pair of sensible shoes
* Realizing you look *exactly* like your driver's license photo

Moments like these can propel an unsuspecting woman into the deep, dark depths of despair known as the **Midlife Crisis,** or **MC.**

The MC has become so commonplace in modern society that, in some upscale neighborhoods, there's a midlife crisis center on every corner. (You can spot these places by the number of Jaguar convertibles and Harley-Davidsons in the parking lot.)

MC is the sudden awareness that your life is more than halfway over and you're running out of time to get it right. It's a time when *men* take stock of their lives and realize they're at least a case short of requisite life experiences like sports cars, silly toupees, and college coeds. So, what do they do? Buy a 'Vette, get a rug, and start dating their daughter's roommates.

A female's midlife crisis is deeper, more complex, and far less expensive. The manifestations can be as diverse as the women themselves:

* Shoulda Woulda Coulda Syndrome
* Career Crisis
* SUV Envy
* Second Puberty
* Elective Surgery Compulsion
* Hysterical Hypochondria

SHOULDA WOULDA COULDA SYNDROME

The midlife woman in crisis is consumed with regrets: things she should've done, opportunities she would've taken, men she could've had while she still had the chance. Obsessed with all the parades that passed her by, she loses herself in the fantasy life she shoulda, woulda, or coulda lived:

* *"If I'd never quit ballet lessons I coulda danced with the Joffrey!"*
* *"I woulda been a country singer if it weren't for those damn cigarettes!"*
* *"Shoulda married that Dr. Kenny Kilgore when I had the chance."*
* *"I coulda been a supermodel if it wasn't for that job at Dairy Queen."*

SUV ENVY

Around the age of forty-one or forty-two, the average woman will wake up to a startling revelation: She's too old for a minivan, too young for a Cadillac, and too fat for a sports car. So what's left? The Sport-Utility Vehicle, or SUV.

SUVs, or "utes," have taken American roads by storm,

and recent studies show that an increasing number of ute drivers are female. Auto manufacturers are keenly aware of this fact. Many have begun marketing to middle-aged women in crisis with models like Pathfinder, Quest, Explorer, and Land Rover.

In the midlifer's warped mind, the SUV can transform even the most dowdy matron into a confident young chick—the "outdoorsy" type of gal who fly-fishes, hikes, reads *Outdoor* magazine, and has an unlimited credit line at Eddie Bauer. Behind the wheel of a ute she "becomes" that woman, wind blowing in her hair, conquering rough off-road terrain . . . even if it's just the speed bumps and potholes of the mall parking lot.

SECOND PUBERTY

Because of the sweeping hormonal changes that accompany midlife (see chapter 3, Menopause and Perimenopause), some women start to experience a kind of puberty déjà vu. This can explain odd behaviors like:

* ❋ Uncontrollable weeping
* ❋ That new wardrobe from Abercrombie & Fitch
* ❋ Wearing body glitter and hair paint to work
* ❋ New phrases like "dude, that rocks" and "he's all that, girlfriend, uh-huh"
* ❋ Hitting on teenage bag boys at the Pak 'N' Save

But the surest sign of second puberty is the tattoo. For reasons unclear to mental-health professionals, a significant percentage of midlife women choose to let big, hairy strangers with pierced lips repeatedly stick ink-filled needles into their skin. Unfortunately, many of these women discover that not only are tattoos *painful*, but they're really meant for young, taut skin. Vivian, a forty-eight-year-old secretary, recalls her first visit to Scarlet Letter Tattoo in St. Paul, Minnesota:

I wanted to do something wild for my fortieth birthday so, after two pitchers of margaritas, a friend and I made our way to the local tattoo parlor. I chose a cute little cupid and had it applied to my right buttock. I felt like a new woman with a sexy secret. My husband loved it, too! Well, eight years and thirty pounds later, that little cupid looks a lot like Willard Scott. Needless to say, I'm getting dressed in the closet these days.

ELECTIVE SURGERY COMPULSION

Thanks to advances in medical technology, skilled surgeons now have the capability to turn Janet Reno into Janet Jackson. Tummy tucks, boob jobs, and liposuction are more accessible and affordable than ever before. This can be a double-edged sword for women who find the idea of physical improvement without dieting and exercise simply irresistible. Because once you start, it's impossible to stop!

Hospital wards are crowded with women who are hopelessly addicted to plastic surgery. Peek under their bandages and you'll find Meg Ryan's nose, Sharon Stone's bottom, Sarah Jessica Parker's stomach, and Pamela Anderson's breasts. Natalie C., a fifty-nine-year-old doctor's wife, explains the lure of the laser:

It's not about vanity or pride or the fountain of youth. Dammit, this is about peer pressure! Competition! My friend gets a nose job, I get my nose and eyelids done. My neighbor gets her breasts done, I do my butt and my thighs. You ask me, "If everybody jumped off a bridge, would you jump, too?" I'd say, "What? And ruin this face?"

HYSTERICAL HYPOCHONDRIA

When a woman reaches a certain age, she naturally becomes more concerned with health and wellness issues. But there are some who cannot read about the latest virus or infectious disease without running to the emergency room in a panic, convinced we have been stricken. This phenomenon is called Hysterical Hypochondria, also known as "sympathy pains." Besides feeling symptoms that aren't there, hysterical hypochondriacs can take a seemingly insignificant condition and turn it into a life-threatening illness:

Sore throat	=	Cancer of the larynx
Sore toe	=	Gangrene
Dry skin	=	Leprosy
Back ache	=	Kidney failure
Stiff legs	=	Polio
Dandruff	=	Psoriasis
Runny nose	=	Cocaine addiction

These women can be found waiting in doctors' offices, clinics, and emergency rooms, clutching copies of the *Physicians' Desk Reference* and *The Mayo Clinic Guide to Really Icky Diseases.* They know the symptoms, incubation periods, transmission methods, and recommended courses of treatment and will recite them at the slightest provocation.

On a positive note, these women are the leading consumers of preplanned funeral packages and make excellent diagnosticians when a doctor is unavailable.

THE TREATMENT

Until medical researchers can find a way to stop the aging process dead in its tracks, the midlife crisis will be an unfortunate fact of life. The best philosophy is to change one's *attitude* about getting older.

As Dr. Ruth Weimaraner explains in her new book, *Midlife, Schmidlife—Just Thank God You're Not Dead!*: "For today's woman, just reaching middle age is a victory! Consider the odds we have beaten in our reckless youth: riding bikes without helmets, driving cars without seat-belts, hitchhiking across Europe, listening to rock and roll at deafening levels, substance use, unprotected sex with multiple partners, jogging without sports bras . . . it's a wonder we're still alive!"

And if that doesn't do it for you, remember: The person who said "Life begins at fifty" is probably dead by now.

Of course, there are severe cases of midlife crisis that cannot be cured by a simple attitude check. For these women, long-term institutionalization at a desert spa where half-naked men "cater" to older women may be required.

CHAPTER 8

WHAT WOULD MARTHA DO? SYNDROME

(WWMDS)

It's a Cult Thing.

THE FACTS

From an early age, Martha Kostyra Stewart set her sights on dominating the domestic landscape of America. As a toddler, she would redecorate her playmates' dollhouses, replacing cheap plastic furniture with real knotty pine cupboards and tiny hand-braided rugs. Her tea parties were legendary. By the age of five, she was commanding twenty-five cents a head for such sold-out lectures as

"Creative Ways to Butter Toast" and "101 Uses for Old Crayon Nubs."

Today, the chairwoman and CEO of Martha Stewart Living Omnimedia has more than she ever dreamed: a magazine, a syndicated TV show, best-selling books . . . and a cultlike discipleship. In fact, after a thorough investigation of her organization, *Mind Control Monthly* placed Martha on its "most dangerous" list of cult leaders, just behind Reverend Sun Myung Moon, "Do" of Heaven's Gate, and Richard Simmons. In that report, experts identified a devastating disorder affecting an estimated 15 percent of Stewart's most ardent followers: **What Would Martha Do? Syndrome,** or **WWMDS.**

Of the 200,000 people said to be afflicted with WWMDS, 90 percent are middle- to upper-class women. (The remaining 10 percent are gay males and Kmart employees.) Victims will exhibit one or more of the following "red-flag" symptoms:

* Obsessive-compulsive use of raffia
* Stockpiling glue guns
* A deliberately "dressed down" appearance
* Sudden, unexplained jaunts to the Connecticut countryside
* Frequent trips to Kmart

* Loitering at airports and other public places
* Social isolation

THE SYMPTOMS

OBSESSIVE-COMPULSIVE USE OF RAFFIA

One of the earliest signs of Martha mind control is the excessive and inappropriate use of raffia. Raffia, a 100 percent natural product obtained from the fronds of the raffia palm in Madagascar, is one of Martha's favorite accoutrements. Shamelessly promoting its use, she uses raffia to wrap hostess gifts, adorn jelly jars, and support gangly plant material. *It is important to remember that raffia use, in moderation, is okay.* But the WWMDS sufferer will cross the line, unable to keep herself from attaching raffia to everything in sight.

Maureen B., a thirty-eight-year-old housewife from Provo, Utah, is a recovering raffia addict:

My raffia abuse started innocently . . . a bouquet of spring flowers here, an autumn wreath there. Soon, I was using every-day. Raffia on the light fixtures, bedposts, toilet-paper rolls, kids' bicycle helmets . . . my own dog wasn't even safe! One night, my husband came in from the garage holding the most mangled mess of raffia I had ever seen. That morning, I had tied little bows on all of his power tools . . . just to surprise him, you know? He said, "For God's sake, Reenie, get some help!" That's when I realized this thing was bigger than me.

The following items should *not* be tied with raffia:
* ❊ Used dental floss
* ❊ Bunches of tampons, no matter how attractively wrapped
* ❊ Family toothbrushes
* ❊ Suppositories
* ❊ Grass

STOCKPILING GLUE GUNS

Another early indicator of WWMDS is the collecting and storing of glue guns, the most important weapon in Martha Stewart's arsenal. Stewart has been known to say, "You can never be too thin, too rich, or have too many glue guns." Her most ardent followers have taken these words to heart.

Again, glue guns, when used in moderation and over a drop cloth or old newspapers, are *not* harmful. But recently, there has been a dramatic increase in glue gun accidents in this country. Glue gun–control proponents support limiting the purchase of glue guns to persons over the age of twenty-one and requiring glue gun registration in all fifty states.

In response, the NGGA (National Glue Gun Association) has recruited Martha Stewart herself as their spokesperson. Slick thirty-second commercials show Martha sporting four glue guns—one in each hand and two in a handmade leather holster slung around her apron. Her message: "All Americans have the inalienable right to bear glue guns. Don't let the actions of a few bumbling fools keep glue guns out of the hands of responsible crafters. Remember: Glue guns don't scald people; people scald people."

In spite of such propaganda, experts say there is no reason for anyone to own more than *two* glue guns, or one per hand.

"DRESSED DOWN" APPEARANCE

As the disease progresses, WWMDS sufferers attempt to identify more closely with their leader by imitating her town-and-country casual style of dress. The "Uniform" makes Marthaphiles easy to recognize:

* Denim shirt with the collar turned up "just so," shirttail untucked
* Khaki pants or white jeans (Memorial Day through Labor Day)

* Rubber "wellies" or garden clogs
* Hand-braided bracelets sporting the letters WWMD?
* Chef's apron or calfskin tool belt
* Coordinating garden gloves or oven mitts

SUDDEN IMPULSE TRIPS TO THE CONNECTICUT COUNTRYSIDE

One of the most disturbing signs of acute WWMDS is the irrepressible urge to visit Connecticut. Each year, hundreds of the faithful make the pilgrimage to rural Westport, leaving family, friends, and careers behind. There, a chosen few receive engraved invitations to the "compound," Martha's pastoral paradise. During an elaborate sit-down luncheon of Coquilles Saint-Jacques and kiwi-raspberry tarts, followers raise their pinkie fingers and swear to:

* Turn over all of their assets, especially the antiques and silver
* Denounce canned vegetables
* Cut ties from friends and family, especially the ones with no taste
* Become a lifetime subscriber to *Martha Stewart Living*

❋   Make no domestic decisions without first asking
    themselves: What Would Martha Do?

Julie B., thirty-six, is a former cult member and
recovering WWMDS victim. She recalls her trip to the
"compound":

*I remember feeling so special after getting my invitation.
Martha had chosen me . . . me from a tract house in Cleveland
. . . to break bread at her eighteenth-century harvest table! When
I arrived that day, Martha came to the door carrying a large
Waterford pitcher on a silver tray. The pitcher was filled to the
brim with a sparkling red liquid. "Kool-Aid?" she asked, then
threw her head back in laughter! And they say Martha doesn't
have a sense of humor! I mean, as if Martha Stewart would ever
dream of serving Kool-Aid to anyone under three years of age!!
Hello?! The beverages were actually wine spritzers made with a
delicate but full-bodied merlot straight from her vineyard. They
made me feel all warm and woozy.*

*   I don't remember much after that . . . except that the vichys-
soise was incredible! She added just a hint of curry . . . anyway,
the next thing I remember was heading home with my party
favor—fresh eggs from Martha's chicken coop in a grapevine bas-
ket she weaved herself that morning. It was then that my nightmare began . . .*

FREQUENT TRIPS TO KMART

After an intense period of indoctrination, the most devoted followers are trained for one-on-one recruiting and sent out into the field. So-called Good Thing Teams are dispatched on a weekly basis to Kmarts all around the country. All recruiters use the same m.o.—chatting up shoppers and steering them over to shelves brimming with Martha Stewart bed linens, towels, and valances.

A typical encounter might go like this:

RECRUITER: Aren't these pinstripe pillow shams the cutest?

RECRUITEE: Mm-hmm. Cute.

RECRUITER: Oh, and I adore the coordinating bed skirt, don't you?

RECRUITEE: Yes. Checks and stripes are good—as long as they're in the complementary colors, of course.

RECRUITER: Do you take Martha's magazine?

RECRUITEE: Oh, I'm not a subscriber. I'll pick it up once in a while.

RECRUITER: The reason I asked is your charming dried-apricot pin. It's just like the one Martha made in the July '97 issue. Did you make it?

RECRUITEE: Um, no . . .

RECRUITER: I'd love to tell you about Martha's latest book, *Tasteful Weddings for Expecting Mothers.* Do you have a minute?

RECRUITEE: Ahem. Well, I don't know.

RECRUITER: We could go over to the snack bar and have a corn dog?

RECRUITEE: No, that's okay—

RECRUITER: I'll buy!

RECRUITEE: Oh, all right.

LOITERING AT AIRPORTS

Good Thing Teams often congregate in airports and other public places, where they beg passersby for spare seashells, driftwood, or other collectibles suitable for crafting. They distribute flyers entitled "The WAY to Bone a Fish" or "Clearing the Path to Heaven with Natural Bristles." Frequently, they spend their Sundays selling seed starters or potting soil on city sidewalks. (A telltale sign of WWMDS is the smell of fresh peat on the hands or clothing.)

SOCIAL ISOLATION

Like Julie B., most WWMDS victims experience a frightening downward spiral three to six months after visiting the compound. Most report feeling alienated from friends and relatives, even those from "good stock." The obsessive compulsion to throw theme parties and harbor barnyard animals in the backyard (home associations be damned) eventually puts people off, creating a lonely existence for followers—alone in their homes with only their quilts and herbed vinegars for comfort. Feeling isolated and overwhelmed from trying to reach standards impossible to attain by anyone but Martha herself, many WWMD victims sink into a bottomless pit of despair.

THE TREATMENT

WWMDS can be cured, but only by a professional exit counselor (formerly known as a "deprogrammer"). Leading an "intervention team" of two or more concerned family members, the EC employs various tactics to "break" the victim's emotional attachment to Martha and her domestic doctrine. Some of the more successful strategies include forcing the subject to:

* Remove all labels from shelves and cupboards
* Bake a cake from a mix
* Eat an entire meal with her salad fork
* Take store-bought potato salad to a pot-luck picnic
* Drink wine from a "bad year"
* Bleach unbleached muslin
* Buy plastic greenery
* Shop at Wal-Mart

While most interventions prove successful, exit counselors may suggest follow-up sessions if needed. Some hardcore cultists can fake a deprogramming long enough to end the intervention, then return to Martha's ways a few months later. For these people, there is no hope.

CHAPTER 9

POST-TRAUMATIC STRESS DISORDER

(PTSD)

THE FACTS

During her lifetime, the average woman will experience anywhere from ten to fourteen certifiably traumatic events. These incidents can be so injurious and potentially damaging that some urban hospitals have opened "emotional trauma centers" for female patients only. The Farrah Fawcett Clinic for Hysterical Women in Los Angeles,

California, is one of the leading facilities in the nation, with celebrities such as Courtney Love and Fran Drescher on their client roster. The Fawcett is setting the standard for the treatment of a devastating syndrome called **Post-Traumatic Stress Disorder,** or **PTSD.** Following are the top seven stressful events that can trigger PTSD.

1. Bad perms
2. The bikini wax
3. Blind dates from hell
4. Baseline mammogram
5. Beanie Baby promotions
6. Road trip with the kids
7. Shopping with Mom

THE SYMPTOMS

BAD PERMS

Every woman feels a sense of trepidation when she hunkers down in her stylist's chair and asks for a new "do." But when a perm is prescribed, warning buzzers go off in the brain. (Danger! Danger! Don King alert! Run away!!) Most women ignore these signals, opting, instead, to let their hair be processed with products so toxic even Dow Chemical wouldn't touch them. These solutions leave the scalp smoldering and smelling like embalming fluid. More often than not, the $90 Shirley Temple ringlets you ordered end up looking like Little Orphan Annie on acid. The end result sends women running for cover and seeking professional help. (Admission records from 1999 show that the Fawcett Clinic saw over 950 women in the Perm Unit. God only knows how many cases of bad perms went untreated.)

THE BIKINI WAX

Dr. Shosanna Wynonna Weinstein of the Fawcett Clinic says some of her most heart-wrenching cases are the post–bikini wax patients: "I see six, maybe seven women a day who have been severely traumatized by negligent bikini waxing. They hobble into the Trauma Unit, legs splayed, clutching their inner thighs. It's a pitiful thing to watch. Sure, we can treat the physical symptoms—a little salve, some cold packs to the groin. But the emotional scars may never heal."

BLIND DATES FROM HELL

Over 30 percent of Post-Traumatic Stress Disorder sufferers are Blind Date from Hell survivors. These women have endured untold indignities caused by some of the most annoying men imaginable. Survivors are tormented by flashbacks of interminable dates with nerds, mama's boys, horn-dogs, and hyperglandular sweat hogs. Stephanie B., a twenty-six-year-old graphic artist, experienced PTSD after a blind date with a data processor:

I have this recurring nightmare. We're sitting in a restaurant after spending four hours at a computer show. I'm in agony. He decides it would be "fun" to order our meal in pig Latin. He insists I do it. "Go ahead," he says. "Eesechay urgerbay with iesfray and a errychay okecay!" Our waitress is not amused. And just to make sure my humiliation is complete, he tells her it's my birthday just to get the free dessert and the "Happy Birthday" song on kazoos. Sometimes when I wake up from that dream, I find myself cowering under a table.

BASELINE MAMMOGRAM

Around the age of forty, a woman will participate in the midlife ritual known as the mammogram. To the uninitiated, the procedure can be highly traumatic. This is especially true for the woman who is not accustomed to having her breasts handled by another female. Not to mention having them kneaded like dough and flattened to the approximate shape of pita bread in an electronic vice.

Cindi K., a forty-one-year-old mother from Iowa, shares a common tale:

The mammography suite in our local hospital was deceptively nice—Laura Ashley wallpaper and drapes, pink pens to fill out the forms. It wasn't nearly as intimidating as the doctor's office . . . not a scale in sight! I didn't even mind the pink paper vest they had me wear! Then my technician entered the room. Helga was a big, strapping gal from Germany with ice-cold hands and sauerkraut on her breath! Apparently, Helga was having a bad day and my boobs were in the right place at the wrong time! Afterward, as I was trying to mold my girls back to their original shape, I heard her say with a smirk in her voice, "You vill come back every year, ya? Is good for you!" To this day, I can't look at a bratwurst without seeing her face.

BEANIE BABY PROMOTIONS

If a Hallmark store with eight hundred square feet of retail space has sixty "Twigs the Giraffe" Beanie Babies to sell and four hundred women show up for the sale, how many people will be maimed or permanently disfigured by the time they reach the cash register?

No matter how you do the math, Beanie Babies are hazardous to your health. In the past five years, emergency room physicians have seen a 16 percent annual increase in Beanie-related injuries. The case log reads like a M.A.S.H. unit's:

* Thirty-five-year-old Caucasian female admitted with puncture wounds to the face and throat after "Bessie the Cow" promotion at Parties4U.

* Twenty-year-old Hispanic female, third-degree lacerations on both hands from "Inky the Octopus" event at Joleen's Hallmark.

* Fifty-nine-year-old African-American female with multiple contusions and internal bleeding, transported by ambulance from "Tuffy the Terrier" Day at Westwind Mall.

You might ask, "Who is perpetrating this vicious brand of Beanie Baby rage?" Dr. Misty Mistenfogen from the Beanie Trauma Center in Detroit, Michigan, has the troubling answer: "*Beanie Baby violence crosses all social, racial, and economic lines. In my twenty-four years of post-trauma experience, I can honestly say that Beanie mania is the only earthly force capable of turning a mild-mannered room mother into a pipe-wielding Tonya Harding.*"

Like post–bikini wax sufferers, victims of Beanie rage will recover physically. But the psychological effects linger. Casualties of the Beanie craze are walking among us, like so many postal workers, ready to snap at the slightest provocation.

ROAD TRIPS WITH THE KIDS

Every year, the Farrah Fawcett Clinic for Hysterical Women sees a marked increase in admissions between

July 4 and Labor Day. The reason? Summer vacations. The family road trip, that perennial ritual that is supposed to be relaxing and invigorating, often drives women to the brink of insanity. Women with road trip–induced PTSD will exhibit the following symptoms:

* Ringing in the ears
* An acute fear of golden arches
* Hearing "voices" that say "Are we there yet?" "How many more minutes?" or "Wendy just puked on the sandwiches!!!"

For these patients, doctors usually prescribe seven days of bed rest in padded isolation suites. Most experts, however, say prevention is the key. Women prone to PTSD are encouraged to avoid family vacations until all members of the family are over twenty-one. Even then, take separate cars.

SHOPPING WITH MOM

Some of the most hard-to-treat cases of PTSD are the women who have survived shopping trips with their mothers. It takes months, sometimes years, for these embattled veterans to recover from the department-store war of wits. Judy W., a twenty-five-year-old physical therapist, recalls her last mother-daughter encounter in a Loehmann's dressing room:

It was an ambush. Mom invited me to lunch for my birthday at my favorite little bistro. Over coffee she says, "And for your present, I'm taking you shopping for that new suit you've wanted! This will be such fun! Just us girls!" Next thing I know, I'm standing in the dressing room in my underwear with twenty suits, five salesladies, and nine unidentified shoppers. They've split into two camps and they're arguing—one for the navy wool crepe and the other for the black matte jersey. I try to slip out in the chaos, but Mom grabs me and says, "You've got such a pretty face. Why can't you pull your hair back once in a while?"

THE TREATMENT

For most PTSD sufferers, experts recommend a simple, laser procedure that zaps the unpleasant experience from memory. In most hospitals, this can be done on an outpatient basis. Side effects may include blurred vision, bloating, and irregular bowel movements. In extreme cases of bad bikini waxes and severe perms, a refund should be demanded.

CHAPTER 10

REUNION NERVOSA

For decades, anthropologists have attempted to explain why otherwise sane, level-headed adults flock to their home-town Holidomes every five or ten years to drink, hug, and "high-five" people who treated them like scum in high school. A perennial institution, the high school reunion is typically a weekend event, organized by the few former cheerleaders who haven't gained weight since graduation. After a long and exhaustive search for former classmates (many of whom joined the witness protection program to escape such events), invitations are issued in school colors:

FRIDAY EVENING:
Icebreaker at The Potted Pig
All-You-Can-Drink
Alums only. Stag. Leave spouses home.
(Mona's orders!!)

SATURDAY AFTERNOON:
Tour of school led by current cheerleaders . . .
(Hands off, Stan!)
Meet at south doors.
(Remove jewelry for metal detectors.)

SATURDAY NIGHT:
Dinner-Dance at Holidome Ballroom
Polynesian buffet / Open bar
Prizes awarded for:
Girl/Boy Who Hasn't Changed a Bit
Girl/Boy with Highest Net Worth
Girl/Boy Still Standing at Midnight

Upon receiving these invitations, men and women respond differently. The man circles the weekend on his calendar, books a flight, and promptly loses the invitation. The woman notes the dates in her planner, calls several airlines to compare fares, books a flight, and promptly has a cow. As the reality of the impending reunion sets in, many women develop a degenerative but temporary disorder called **Reunion Nervosa.**

Reunion Nervosa, or RN, is a disease that progresses in five stages:

* Denial
* Anger
* Bargaining
* Depression
* Acceptance

THE SYMPTOMS

DENIAL

This stage usually occurs within moments of receiving the reunion invitation. Although the proof is right there in crimson and gold, the woman refuses to believe what she sees in front of her:

"It can't be twenty years already! I just finished my acne treatment last month!"

"There's gotta be some mistake. There must be another Mary Alice Bumgardner from New Castle Academy, Class of '73."

"But we just had a high school reunion. I still have the hickeys on my neck to prove it!"

During this stage a woman will withdraw from society, refraining from normal activities. Searching for any stimuli that will distract her attention from the invitation, she'll revert to the comfort of old habits. This will last approximately two to four days, or until the Ben & Jerry's runs out.

ANGER

In this stage, the woman is furious and looking to place blame:

"How did they find me? I've been divorced three times and have an unlisted number . . . who are they, the FBI?"

"Damn that cheerleader-from-hell Buffy Lou Pertbottom! She knows I just had a baby six years ago! Just because she's got the same anorexic size-three butt doesn't mean she can rub my nose in it! She doesn't think I've got the nerve to come. Well, I'll show her . . ."

In many cases, anger breeds defiance and the Reunion Nervosa victim will find herself checking the "Yes, this Mustang will be there" box on the RSVP card.

BARGAINING

Now the woman makes a deal with God:

"If you help me lose forty pounds in the next month, I promise to return all those Mel Gibson movies to Blockbuster."

"Just a small promotion to vice president, God, and I'll never take so much as a paper clip from the office."

"I'm just asking for a minor tornado, Lord. Just enough to cause structural damage to the Holidome. Nobody has to die."

Of course, all the bargaining in the world won't stop a reunion by divine intervention. (Although there *was* an incident in Iowa in which a livestock train derailed, cutting a path of destruction and cow dung through the Cedar Hollow Holidome just minutes before the Class of '78 was scheduled to arrive for the Cornshucker Gala.) As the reunion date nears, reality sinks in.

DEPRESSION

Unlike men, who, on the maturation curve, have nowhere to go but *up* after high school, a woman with Reunion Nervosa faces a disturbing possibility:

Maybe I peaked too soon?

This fear is compounded by masochistic "trips down memory lane"—browsing through old yearbooks, photos, programs, love letters—all tangible reminders that she'll never be better looking than she was at seventeen. This startling realization catapults the woman into a deep, dark depression for which the only cure is: **Old Boyfriend Validation,** or **OBV.**

One of the ways a woman can reassure herself that she's "still got it" is if her old boyfriend still finds her attractive. *This is the litmus test of many a Reunion Nervosa sufferer.* By redirecting her energy onto the Old Boyfriend, she snaps out of her funk and enters the last stage of the disease: acceptance.

ACCEPTANCE

Now the woman has a focus. A goal, if you will. She sets her sights on dazzling the Old Boyfriend with her wit, her sense of self, and a new outfit she can't afford or fit into. It doesn't matter if he is fat, married with six kids, bald, toothless, or just getting by on a carhop's wages. If the Old Boyfriend utters the words "You haven't changed a bit," the reunion will be a success. Now the only thing to do is lose thirty pounds, highlight the hair, and get a facial peel.

ACUTE COUNTDOWN NERVOSA

As the reunion looms closer, the RN sufferer becomes immersed in what experts call the "New Old Me" mode. In a fruitless attempt to turn back the swelling hands of time, a woman will exhibit classic Reunion Nervosa symptoms:

* Crash dieting
* Makeover mania
* Nostalgic wardrobe planning

CRASH DIETING

About four weeks prior to the reunion, the RN victim will subject her body to horrendous abuse—liquid diets, three-hour sauna baths, and Richard Simmons's *Sweatin' to the Oldies* videos—all in a futile attempt to get down to her high school weight. Tragically, most women don't realize that in 1991, in accordance with the Involuntary Metric Conversion Act, all U.S. scales were recalibrated to weigh 25 pounds (or 11.34 kilograms) *heavier.* That means that a woman who weighed 125 pounds in 1973 but weighs 150 pounds *today* . . . hasn't gained an ounce. Unfortunately, most women don't get this information in time.

MAKEOVER MANIA

Every Saturday, department-store cosmetic counters are crowded with ladies having their faces made over by Tammy Faye Bakker look-alikes in pastel lab coats. In-store surveys indicate that 79 percent of these consumers have a high school reunion to attend within one week of the makeover, if not that same night.

As any beleaguered cosmetic consultant will attest, many of these shoppers have unrealistic expectations about what makeup can and cannot do. The most popular requests are:

* Cheekbones like Audrey Hepburn's
* Brows like Brooke Shields's
* Lips like Julia Roberts's
* Eyes like Uma Thurman's
* A natural blush like Monica Lewinsky's

After dropping $300, $400, even $500, a woman will leave the store with a makeup kit that rivals RuPaul's. Unfortunately, when the woman attempts to apply the products herself, she often winds up looking exactly *like* RuPaul. This can cause confusion at the reunion when the only drag queen expected to attend is the former Show Tune Society president, Kip Kilroy.

NOSTALGIC WARDROBE PLANNING

Occasionally, two or more women will get together and decide it would be "fun" to dress up and attend the reunion their wearing old:

* Pep club uniforms

* Bell bottoms and halter tops
* Prom dresses
* Hot pants
* Navy blazers and pleated skirts (Catholic school only)

This is an example of "co-dependent reunion nervosa," an offshoot of "co-dependent rest room visitation." It is *never* a good idea!!

THE TREATMENT

One of the most successful techniques in the treatment of Reunion Nervosa is the "reunion rehearsal." This is when a person will actually "practice" by attending a random reunion of an unknown school. After registering at the name-tag table under an assumed name, the woman can move among the crowd, unfettered by old stereotypes, associations, or disapproving boyfriends. Only then will she realize the universal truths of high school reunions:

* Women age *much* more gracefully than men.
* The cheerleaders are still perky.
* You dumped the Old Boyfriend for a damn good reason.

CHAPTER 11

THELMA
AND LOUISE
SYNDROME

(TALS)

THE FACTS

In the days of the early settlers, a woman's place was in the homestead. Except for a weekly jaunt into town for sugar, flour, lard, and a cholesterol check, the pioneer woman never escaped the bosom of her family. Not for one blessed moment.

That changed, however, when Bessie LaMont from Cogsville, Ohio, invented an ingenious plot to get herself and her friends away from the watchful eyes of their husbands. She called it the quilting bee. Held behind closed doors in the local church, the bee was a ladies-only affair featuring idle gossip, raucous sex talk, and, just to cover their rears, quilting. Bessie's bees were notoriously wild, sometimes continuing until well after eight o'clock. Occasionally, passersby could hear women inside the church hollering things like, "Whoop-ti-do!" and "Do tell, Modesta, do tell!" These were the first recorded Girls Nights Out in history.

As generations passed, women continued to find creative ways to escape the confines of hearth and home. In the '60s, companies like Mary Kay cosmetics and Tupperware caught on to the trend and cashed in with the following marketing strategy: Get a woman out of the house. Give her wine and Rice Krispies Treats. Exfoliate her pores. Burp a lettuce keeper, whatever. She'll be so grateful, she'll buy anything!

Today, Girls Nights Out are so common that, on any night in any given city, you can walk into a bar and spot a group of women, martinis in hand, singing "Baby Love" on the dance floor. This behavior is caused by a temporary neurological disorder called **TALS,** or **Thelma and Louise Syndrome.**

TALS occurs when otherwise sane, stable, and well-behaved women feel an uncontrollable compulsion to leave their homes and behave like teenagers, tramps or, in extreme cases, men.

The three most common manifestations of TALS are:

THE BACHELORETTE PARTY

The feminine counterpart to the "stag party," this event marks the last time a bride-to-be can behave like a soused sorority girl and get away with it. A well-executed bachelorette party can turn the holiest of rollers into a harlot. That's why the tradition is so popular. The parties usually follow a common itinerary:

7:00 P.M.	Convene at restaurant for dinner.
7:01–7:10	Scream, hug, order cocktails.
7:10–7:20	Admire new outfits, haircuts, bride's engagement ring.
7:20–8:00	Order cocktails, bash men.
8:00–9:00	Order dinner and wine, absolve each other for breaking diets.
9:00–10:00	Dessert drinks all around, bash men.
10:00–10:15	Move to club across town, bashing men in transit.
10:15–11:00	Order cocktails. Bride opens gifts—edible underwear, sex toys, and coasters (there's always a practical one in the bunch).

11:00–1:00   Chippendales floor show. Scream, ogle, and paw male strippers. Stuff a week's salary in the black guy's G-string.

THE DIVORCE PARTY

When it comes to rallying the troops in an emergency, women are brigadier generals. And when a fellow female gets divorced, her friends will be there en masse with a sympathetic ear and plenty of booze, Kleenex, and chocolate.

The Divorce Party typically follows the same itinerary as the Bachelorette Party (see previous page) with three notable exceptions:

1. The guest of honor leaves her ring at home;
2. Nobody gives coasters to a divorced woman; and
3. Somebody always tries to take the black guy home.

THE DIVA WEEKEND

As the disease advances, some TALS sufferers are no longer satisfied by the occasional night out. The Diva Weekend is an extended Girls Night Out usually involving wilder nights, hotel shenanigans, and unconstrained shopping in big, cosmopolitan cities. In New York's Rockefeller Plaza, you can always spot diva weekenders vying for face time on the *Today* show. Perfectly coifed but slightly dazed from the night before, these are the women wearing foam Statue of Liberty crowns and holding signs that say "Hi, kids! Send money! Spent traveler's checks on bail!"

The following behaviors are associated with TALS:
* Excessive liquor consumption
* Nonsmoker smoking
* Girl-girl dancing
* Karaoke compulsion

THE SYMPTOMS

EXCESSIVE LIQUOR CONSUMPTION

The main ingredient of a night out with the *boys* is beer. Men can't seem to enjoy anything—football, poker, strippers, professional wrestling—without a brewski in hand. Women tend to be more discriminating, choosing a beverage that will complement the occasion:

Engagement = wine or champagne

Divorce = martinis

Diva Weekend = mimosas (breakfast);

Bloody Marys (lunch); martinis (happy hour),

wine (dinner); whatever the bartender is pouring
for the rest of the night

NONSMOKER SMOKING

In 1985, U.S. Surgeon General C. Everett Koop presented
some startling statistics from a $7 million federal study
conducted by the tobacco lobby. The study revealed that
there are approximately 1.5 million "nonsmoking"
women who, when exposed to female smokers in liquor-
oriented environments, will light up and puff like the
chimneys of London. Girls Night Out smokers cite the
following rationalizations for their unhealthy behavior:

* "I only smoke when I drink."
* "The other girls made me do it."
* "But I didn't inhale."

Afraid of being discovered and admonished by their
vigilante children, these women hide their tobacco usage
with gum, perfume, and curiously strong breath mints.

GIRL-GIRL DANCING

When the amount of liquor consumed exceeds a
woman's maximum-intake limit, the TALS victim will
lose her inhibitions and succumb to the temptations of
girl-girl dancing. For many women, same-sex dancing is

no big deal. They've been doing it, by default, since junior high. But even the most conservative woman who believes dancing should always be a male-female activity will bolt to the dance floor like a lesbian on Ecstacy when certain songs are played.

In an experiment conducted by the Radcliffe Institute for the Advanced Study of Girl-Girl Dancing, researchers found that 87 percent of all heterosexual women, after consuming an average of 2.8 cocktails, will knowingly dance without male partners to the following songs:

* "Disco Inferno"
* "Devil with the Blue Dress On"
* "Stop, in the Name of Love"
* "I Will Survive"
* "Maggie May"
* "Yummy, Yummy, Yummy—I've Got Love in My Tummy"
* "Hey Mickey, You're So Fine, You're So Fine You Blow My Mind"

KARAOKE COMPULSION

Like girl-girl dancing, a turn at the karaoke microphone can prove irresistible to a woman under the influence of TALS. Again, peer pressure and liquor consumption come into play as a woman will, against her better judgment, humiliate herself on stage in a roomful of strangers with an off-key rendition of "The Way We Were" or "Crazy." Statistics show that 90 percent of all karaoke experiences end badly, with flashbacks often continuing for years after the performance.

Recently, a national karaoke awareness organization, Citizens for KRAP (Karaoke Reform and Prohibition), recently launched a bumper-sticker campaign targeting women on Girls Nights Out. Their slogan:

FRIENDS DON'T LET FRIENDS SING KARAOKE!

THE TREATMENT

Under normal circumstances, Thelma and Louise Syndrome will run its course and dissipate at the conclusion of the girls-only event. In rare cases, however, a Girls Night Out or Diva Weekend can turn TALS into a permanent state of mind. In these extreme cases, doctors recommend that women steer clear of country-western bars, Brad Pitt, and the Grand Canyon.

CHAPTER 12

DR. LAURANOIA

DL

THE FACTS

Since Laura Schlessinger, Ph.D., hit the airwaves with her own brand of "preach, teach, and nag," she has amassed thousands of loyal listeners, sold scads of books, and launched countless women on one-way guilt trips. Syndicated on over five hundred radio stations, the good "doctor" (the Ph.D. is in physiology) gets over two hundred thousand calls a day from people desperately seeking answers to life's pressing questions, such as:

* Should I marry my drug-addict boyfriend while I'm still pregnant or wait till he's out of jail?

* Is it fair for me to hold a grudge against my step-father just because he strangled my cat?
* Will my husband get upset if my old boyfriend comes to live with us for a few months while he's on probation?
* Am I morally obligated to be in my best friend's wedding if I object to the color of the brides-maids' dresses?
* How can I get my family to respect my Wiccan beliefs?

Only a few dozen callers actually make the cut each day. For the chosen few, Dr. Laura doles out morally correct advice and thought-provoking questions on the air, the gist of which is always: "Lady, how stupid can you get?" Dr. Laura dishes "dumb" like Martha Stewart dishes soup. And, like Stewart's followers, Schlessinger's devotees are willing to subject themselves to the most brutal and relentless abuse.

Recently, scientists at the Center for the Study of Mean People as Role Models have begun to research the Dr. Laura phenomenon. By studying some of the doctor's most ardent followers in double-blind, longitudinal stud-ies from the prone position, experts have identified a behavioral disorder that appears to be reaching epidemic proportions in this country: **Dr. Lauranoia.**

THE SYMPTOMS

Classified as a subheading under the psychological classi-
fication "post-traumatic browbeating by a radio personality," Dr. Lauranoia is the overwhelming and irrational
fear that everything you have ever done in your whole
life is stupid. Because according to Dr. Laura, nine out of
ten women are dumber than dirt. In fact, stupid is Dr.
Laura's specialty. That's why the word appears in the titles
of so many of her books:

   * *Ten Stupid Things Women Do to Mess Up Their Lives*
   * *Ten Stupid Things Men Do to Mess Up Their Lives*
   * *I'm O.K., You're Stupid*
   * *Chicken Soup for the Stupid Soul*
   * *Don't Sweat the Stupid Stuff*
   * *Little Stupid Women*
   * *Men Are from Dumb, Women Are from Stupid*

Most victims of Dr. Lauranoia are regular listeners who
live vicariously through the people they hear on the show.
They take the callers' moral dilemmas to heart and listen
with guilty fascination as the doctor moves in for the kill:

DR. LAURA: *Mirna, welcome to the program.*

MIRNA: *Hi, Dr. Laura. I think you're the best thing
              since God.*

DR. LAURA: *Naturally. But what can I help you with?*

MIRNA: *Well, I am my kid's mom.*

DR. LAURA: *Excellent. A boy bushkin or a girl bushkin?*

MIRNA: *What's a bushkin?*

DR. LAURA: *What, are you stupid? I mean, three morons
              with a collective IQ of thirty-four would know
              what a bushkin is! Don't tell me. You're a
              product of public school.*

MIRNA: *Well, actually—*

DR. LAURA: *Bushkin, baby, kidlet! Like my bushkin,
              Deryk. He said the cutest thing the other day.
              He said, "Mom, when I grow up I want to be
              just like you . . . except with smaller hair and
              no boobies." I was all verklempt!*

MIRNA: *Anyway, the other day my baby-sitter was—*

DR. LAURA: *Excuse me. You said* you *were your kid's mom.*

MIRNA: *Yes, he's five—*

DR. LAURA: *I'm sorry. I don't understand. You can't say you're your kid's mom if you have a baby-sitter.*

MIRNA: *Oh but I am, Dr. Laura. I have the T-shirt and everythi—*

DR. LAURA: *Wait just a minute. You didn't hear me? I just said, "You can't say 'I am my kid's mom' and have a baby-sitter." It's against the rules. Didn't the screener tell you that?*

MIRNA: *But, I just—*

DR. LAURA: *Lew! Fire the screener! Obviously, Mirna, you are just another pathetic product of the left-wing, feminist movement who thinks it's just fine and dandy to go around saying "I am my kid's mom" when they have a baby-sitter. Deryk never had a baby-sitter. Hang up. Hang up and go think about what you have just said, you filthy, disgusting slut. . . . Now go take on the day!*

Listeners view these drubbings like a car wreck—you know you shouldn't look, but you just can't help it. Such sadomasochistic tendencies are common in Dr. Lauranoiacs, as only the severely afflicted can listen to brutal tongue-lashings over day care, divorce, and "shack-up studs" for hours on end.

Soon, Lauranoiacs adopt defense mechanisms in a feeble attempt to convince themselves that they are not as stupid as the poor saps who call the show. Some examples of this behavior are:

* ❊ Memorizing the "Ten Stupid Things"
* ❊ Pointing out to friends which of the "Ten Stupid Things" they are guilty of
* ❊ Purchasing a week's worth of "Go Take On the Day" T-shirts
* ❊ Introducing themselves at cocktail parties with "I am my kid's mom"
* ❊ Picketing day-care centers
* ❊ Quoting Dr. Laura's books like Bible passages

There are a few women, however, whose disease progresses to the most advanced stages. These are the callers who actually get on the air with the doctor herself. If they survive the call at all (the mortality rate for Dr. Laura callers is 47 percent), these women often become scarred for life by such a terrifying event. Maria, a thirty-four-year-old single mother of two, has only recently recovered from a call to Dr. Laura in 1997:

I summoned the courage to dial the number. My husband had left me for a stripper who happened to be my mother. I wanted to know if it was okay to move five hundred miles away and tell my five-year-old that her daddy and grandma exploded in a freak grain-elevator accident. I started to tell the screener my moral dilemma. But all she wanted to do was ask me questions like "On a scale of one to ten, how much do you admire Dr. Laura?" and "Do you have a baby-sitter? Because if the answer is 'yes,' you may not say 'I am my kid's mom' on the air. Do you understand?" Suddenly, as she was asking how many T-shirts and mugs I wanted to buy, I heard a click! Then, it was Dr. Laura's voice. "Maria, welcome to the program." After that, it's a blur. I can only remember remnants of what she said: "day care bad . . . kids need a father . . . take their grandma away . . . selfish . . . lady, how stupid can you get?" Afterward, she told me to order two books, subscribe to her newsletter, and say three Hail Marys and four Our Fathers.

In the aftermath of such trauma, these pitiful souls will often develop a debilitating condition much like the fallout experienced by Vietnam vets and survivors of the

Cabbage Patch riots of '79. Hospitalization is sometimes required to treat symptoms such as:

* Flashbacks (particularly on anniversary dates: one week, month, or year after the call)
* Sleep disturbances (typically talking in one's sleep: "I am my kid's mom! I am! I am!")
* Depression
* Being easily startled (especially upon hearing "New Attitude" by Patti LaBelle)

THE TREATMENT

The best treatment, of course, is prevention. Total abstinence from Dr. Laura is the only sure cure of Dr. Lauranoia. The course of recovery is difficult, even one day at a time. Addicts will fall "off the wagon" and attempt once more to contact the doctor for their masochistic pleasures. For these patients, the priority is damage control. It is vital to remember the following guidelines:

Ten Stupid Things Women Do When Calling Dr. Laura

1. Fail to tell Dr. Laura she's the greatest thing since sliced bread.
2. Accidently mention "those Internet pictures."

3.   Forget to say "I am my kid's mom."

4.   Neglect to say "I value your opinion."

5.   Dare to say "pardon me" or "huh?" when you don't hear what Dr. Laura says the first time . . . because you get one chance to benefit from Dr. Laura's infinite wisdom and that's *it*, understand?

6.   Innocently ask why she calls herself "doctor" in this context when her Ph.D. is in physiology.

7.   Ask for the name of the lawyer who handled her divorce.

8.   Use phrases like "low self-esteem," "lack of communication," or other terms Dr. Laura considers left-wing psychobabble.

9.   Call Deryk a mama's boy.

10.   Suggest she submit that hairdo to *Glamour*'s "Dos and Don'ts" column.

CHAPTER 13

DRAMA
QUEEN
DISORDER

(DQD)

THE FACTS

From 69 to 30 B.C. Cleopatra, Queen of Egypt, starred in her own ancient soap opera, called *As the Nile Churns* by the locals. At eighteen, she married her brother, Ptolemy XIII, a much younger man of twelve. This wasn't quite as scandalous as one might think since, in those days, it was common for siblings to wed. It kept the guest list from getting out of hand.

Then Cleo, with the help of Julius Caesar, revolted

against her husband and conquered his kingdom for the Romans. When Ptolemy XIII tragically died on a Roman holiday with Audrey Hepburn, the Queen married another brother, Ptolemy XIV, while having an illicit affair with Caesar. She eventually bore Caesar's child and, taking great care to hide the indiscretion from her subjects, named the boy Ptolemy Caesar, or "Caesar" for short. Cleopatra moved the child to Rome and secretly taught him the family trade—making salads from romaine lettuce, Parmesan cheese, egg, and anchovies. Returning to Egypt after the assassination of Big Caesar over some stale croutons, she met Marc Antony and fell in love. Cleopatra and Marc married in 36 B.C. and attempted to regain power in Egypt by tainting all salads in the kingdom with salmonella. Failing at that attempt, Antony and Cleopatra killed themselves by suffocating each other with their togas.

Cleopatra's was the first recorded case of **Drama Queen Syndrome,** or **DQS,** in history. Since then, women with DQS have multiplied in great numbers— holding court in offices, locker rooms, beauty salons . . . anywhere that provides an opportunity to rant, rave, whine, or gush to a captive audience.

Drama Queen Syndrome is a pervasive and conta- gious disorder known to strike women at any age, but particularly at thirteen. Simply defined, DQS is a bio-hormonal, neurophysical defect that causes "normal" women to behave like Erica Kane. Symptoms include:

* Exaggerated syllabic emphasis (i.e., "This is the most *fab*-ulous dinner I've *ev*-er *had*, dahling!")
* Dramatic entrances and exits
* Tragicomic storytelling
* Tantrums

THE SYMPTOMS

EXAGGERATED SYLLABIC EMPHASIS

One of the most flagrant signs of DQS is an affected speech pattern in which consonants and vowels are accented or drawn out. Drama queens speak in *italics* with a minimum of three exclamation points per sentence. For example:

* You *can't* be *se*rious!!!
* It's a *trage*dy, I tell you!!!
* Can you be*lieve* it? They didn't have ver*mouth*!!!
* I'm *soooooo* exh*haaaaauuuus*ted!!!

DQS causes women to speak several decibel levels above that of the average female voice. This puts the volume range somewhere between Ethel Merman's and Richard Simmons's.

DRAMATIC ENTRANCES AND EXITS

As the disease progresses, women with DQS will actually
lose the ability to walk. Instead, they glide, sashay, strut,
storm, creep, leap, march, and rumba. Likewise, drama
queens are physically incapable of simply entering a room.
They feel compelled to make *grand* entrances. In fact,
women in the advanced stages of the disease will go to
great lengths to *plan* their entrances—days, sometimes
months in advance—as dictated by the following guidelines:

1. Obtain blueprints of location to determine opti-
   mal door through which to enter for maximum
   impact.[1]
2. Check lighting.
3. Secure traffic-stopping outfit, flashy enough to
   cause a stir but not enough to draw criticism.
4. Be "fashionably late" by at least thirty minutes.
5. Choose and memorize suitably impressive opening line like: "Salutations and hi, even!"

The entrance is always followed by a series of indi-
vidual greetings, punctuated by indiscriminate hugs and
air kisses. The main objective is for the entrance to be the

[1] In 1999, the Drama Queens with Disabilities Act provided that all public entryways and doors be adapted for easy accessibility, complimentary
color schemes, and flattering lighting.

best of the evening. Should anyone attempt an entrance after hers, the DQ launches a pre-emptive strike, greeting the latecomer before she can utter a word:

> *"Don't* tell *me! Those have* got *to be* Prada *you're wearing!* Come*! Sit! And show me those a*dor*able shoes!"*

With tactics like this, no one else has a chance.

Just as important as the entrance, the exit is a DQ's chance to make a lasting impression. Effective exit lines are of the essence, and women with DQS will rehearse them for hours at a time to perfect the intonation and sincerity level:

> *"*Ba-*bye!!! We* must *get together!!!* Call *me!!!"*
>
> *"Let's do* lunch*!!! My treat,* Real*ly!!! I* promise *I'll show* up *this time!!!"*
>
> *"I'll* die *if you don't give me that* can*ape recipe!!! Tuna and cheese on* toast *points . . . you're an absolute gour*mand*!!!"*

TRAGICOMIC STORYTELLING

Women with DQ will go to any lengths to milk their time in the spotlight. A seasoned drama queen can turn a brief humorous anecdote about, say, burning the Thanksgiving turkey into a thirty-minute stand-up comedy routine:

"And [starting to snicker], this is the funny part [chuckling, one-minute dramatic pause], just as I was [laughing] . . . just as I was taking the turkey out of the oven [hysterically laughing for three minutes] . . . oh, I don't know if I can [more laughing, deep breath, two-minute dramatic pause] . . . anyway, as I was taking the silly thing out, I looked up [losing it, on her knees, barely breathing—seven minutes] . . . I'm sorry [gasping] . . . I looked up and [gut-busting laughter—four minutes] . . . and there was Mom [cackling like a lunatic now—five minutes] . . . and she said [two-minute dramatic pause] 'Julia, *darling, this* is a *cornish game hen*!' "

By the same token, the DQS-afflicted woman will apply similar histrionics to a sad story, typically about romance gone sour. The average length of a DQ's "breakup story" is two hours, usually occurring in the ladies room of a bar. The longest "breakup story" ever recorded was seven hours, on October 27, 1997, at a Houlihan's restaurant in Chicago, Illinois. At 5:30 that evening, twenty-nine-year-old Dede McWalters and two companions were seen entering the women's rest room. Hours passed. Not a sign of the three friends. Throughout the night, diners noticed waitresses carrying appetizers, three Fettuccini Primaveras and eighteen Long Island Iced Teas through the rest room doors. Dede and her friends finally emerged at 1:00 A.M.

Dede was notably composed. One of her companions, however, had to be hospitalized overnight.

Next to the breakup story, the "personal injury or ill-ness story" is the drama queen's specialty. Women with DQS are happiest when they have been deathly ill or critically injured, particularly when they have a cast, scar, or neck brace to show for their trouble.

TANTRUMS

The temper tantrum is a classic symptom of acute Drama Queen Syndrome. Similar to the emotional breakdown of a toddler in her "terrible twos," a DQS-induced tantrum is a frightful display of anger featuring deafening screeching, uncontrollable sobbing, and, in Texas, death threats against cheerleaders or their mothers.

The following events can spontaneously provoke a tantrum:

* A broken fingernail
* Rain
* Flat soda pop
* Cold coffee

WARNING: DQS tantrums can be dangerous, even life-threatening. Experts recommend immediate evacuation by onlookers when a tantrum occurs. Cases have been reported of bystanders injured by flailing hands, especially when the fingernails have been manicured to a fine point.

THE TREATMENT

For years, medical researchers had suspected a genetic link for Drama Queen Syndrome because of its tendency to run in families—daughters, mothers, grandmothers, kooky aunts from the old country. Recent laboratory tests have identified the gene that causes DQS. (Ironically, it was right next to the gene that causes black roots in blondes.) While the procedure has yet to be perfected, scientists can now remove the DQS gene in utero and replace it with a "placebo gene," giving women more of an "even keel" personality, like Janet Reno's.

CHAPTER 14

ROAD RAG

(The Feminine Equivalent
of Road Rage)

In the past decade, most Americans have become painfully aware of the cultural phenomenon known as Road Rage. These episodes of vehicular violence include physical threats, forcing drivers off the road, gunfire, and, worst of all, malicious mooning. Generally perpetrated by frustrated, type-A personalities, road rage is triggered by simple acts of discourtesy:

* Changing lanes without signaling
* Tailgating
* Excessive honking
* Driving too slow

And, in California:

✳   Failing to yield to a drive-by shooting

Historically, most road warriors have been men. The California Council for the Peaceful Co-existence of Automobiles (CCPCA) estimates nineteen out of twenty incidents of Road Rage involve male-against-male violence. And while they aren't totally immune, females tend to exhibit a less vehement version of Road Rage called **Road Rag.**

Defined as "a passive-aggressive combination of suppressed rage and relentless nagging," Road Rag is the kinder, gentler response to stressful driving conditions. While a man thinks nothing of chasing down and pulverizing a guy just for cutting him off at the exit, a woman will bitch to herself from behind rolled-up windows so the offender has zero chance of hearing her.

Take this quiz to see if you might suffer from Road Rag:

1. When another driver follows me too closely, I:

    A. Slam on my brakes, hoping he'll smash into my rear end so I can sue the S.O.B. for whiplash.

    B. Pull over and flip him the bird while he passes.

    C. Slow down to geriatric speed, lecture him

under my breath, and hope he gets the message that he's annoying me.

2. When somebody continues honking at me for no apparent reason, I:

   A. Blast my horn and try to out-honk him.

   B. Throw up both hands as if to say, "What the hell can I do?"

   C. Cuss at him under my breath, give him "the look," and hope he gets the message that he's annoying me.

3. When the driver in front of me changes lanes without signaling, I:

   A. Roll down my window and shout every obscenity I can think of.

   B. Lay on the horn and tailgate him for at least a mile.

   C. Scold him under my breath, flash my warning lights, and hope he gets the message that he's annoying me.

If you answered C to any of the above questions, you are probably already suffering from Road Rag.

Women with this disorder will exhibit strange, often bizarre behavior behind the wheel, including:

✱ Under-the-breath ranting

* Driver-passenger transference
* The discreet middle-finger flip-off
* Intentional old-lady driving

THE SYMPTOMS

UNDER-THE-BREATH RANTING

When you see a woman muttering to herself in a car, chances are she's experiencing an episode of Road Rag. Provoked by an annoying driver, the ragger will berate the perpetrator in harsh but hushed tones, using profane language though barely moving her lips:

"What do you think you're doing, $%&$@#%? Who taught you to ★&%$!#@ drive? Are you &%#$#^ blind? What about my bumper do you find so &%##$ attractive? Oh, that's just great, now move over into the &%$%# left lane and go around me. Far be it from me to slow you down, mister big important &★%$@% businessman . . ."

Having purged the tension of the moment, the woman will pull up next to the offender at a stoplight and nod to him, smiling as if there's nothing wrong.

DRIVER-PASSENGER TRANSFERENCE

When a woman with Road Rag is irritated, she often will transfer her frustrations onto the nearest available person— the passenger. This type of ragging is usually presented as a string of accusatory rhetorical questions no one in the car could possibly answer. Nor should they try:

"Who does this guy think he is? It's all about him, isn't it? He's just got to be first, doesn't he? And when's the last time they paved this road? Do you think these bumps are helping my suspension? Is this why I pay my taxes? What is he honking for? So now I don't have a right to drive in the passing lane? Uh-oh! Someone call the lane monitor!"

THE DISCREET MIDDLE-FINGER FLIP-OFF

Unlike her type-A counterparts, the Road Ragger cannot bring herself to flip off another driver, no matter how obnoxious the offense. This is because most women were brought up to believe that obscene gestures are rude and unladylike and, therefore, should be performed only by rude and unladylike men. Frustrated by the double standard, some women have invented sly ways of disguising the flip-off as an innocuous gesture:

❋ Scratching the cheek with the middle finger

* Picking the nose with the middle finger
* Adjusting the side mirror with the middle finger
* Hand-signaling a right turn with the middle finger

Though the other driver might be clueless as to her intent, the Road Ragger still derives relief from having made the gesture.

INTENTIONAL OLD-LADY DRIVING

In the heat of vehicular one-upsmanship, old-lady driving can do more to irritate a rival driver than any other Road Rag tactic. This strategy is typically used by a Road Ragger when she is being tailgated. Slowing to a crawl, she weaves back and forth over the middle line and applies her brakes every twenty feet, all the while dressing down the other driver under her breath.

This is classic passive-aggressive Road Rag behavior that can irritate other drivers to distraction.

THE TREATMENT

Research has shown that women with chronic Road Rag can develop high blood pressure, heart palpitations, and hemorrhoids as a result of suppressed rage. That is why some physicians prescribe an aggressive course of therapy, including testosterone injections and behavior modification, for the treatment of Road Rag. Using computerized driving simulators, the woman behind the wheel is abused, threatened, honked at, and rear-ended until she is forced to act out—blaring her horn, flipping off drivers, and cussing just like a man.

CHAPTER 15

POSTPARTUM DEPRESSION

PPD

THE FACTS

In 460 B.C., a up 'n' coming Greek physician named Hippocrates observed the strange behavior of postnatal women in his village: moaning, complaining, and stoning random passersby. Chalking it up to primitive birthing methods and the lack of cable TV, he dismissed this as "normal postnatal response," although he alluded to the phenomenon in his famous "Hippocratic Oath":

I swear by Apollo the physician, by Asclepius, . . . and by all the gods and goddesses, that, according to my ability and judg-

ment, I will keep this oath . . . according to the law of medicine but to no others except personal injury and medical malpractice attorneys. I will follow that system of regimen which, according to my ability and judgment, I consider for the benefit of my patients, and abstain from whatever is deleterious and mischievous except on Wednesdays and Thursdays, when I'm on the golf course. I will give no deadly medicine to anyone if asked, nor suggest any such counsel; and in like manner I will not give to a new mother any sharp object, heavy stone, or, God forbid, battering ram.

The modern medical community was puzzled by that last part until the American Psychiatric Association officially recognized the condition to which Hippocrates referred in the 1994 edition of *The Diagnostic and Statistical Manual of Mental Disorders We Can't Explain.* They called it **Postpartum Depression,** or **PPD.**

Occurring to some degree in an estimated 70 percent of new mothers, PPD is a slow or sudden realization of any or all of the following:

* ✳ You'll never be able to sit down again without wincing.
* ✳ Forty-five minutes a pop is all you're gonna get in the sleep department for the rest of your life.
* ✳ You're going to smell like sour milk and poo-poo for the next two years.

* You cannot tell where your breasts end and your stomach begins.
* You're so tired you can't remember your middle name.
* Natural childbirth is a crock.
* Your sex life is over . . .
* . . . and you don't care.

In the face of such self-evident truths, who wouldn't be depressed?

The onset of PPD varies from mother to mother. Some women experience their first symptoms the moment they attempt to use the hospital toilet for the first time. This single event can send the postpartum woman into a terrifying downward spiral. Surprisingly, it's not the excruciating physical pain of moving from bed to bathroom that causes distress. It's the rest-room mirror, bathed in harsh fluorescent light, which reflects another inescapable truth: that expectant mother's glow you had two days ago has burned out like a cheap forty-watt bulb.

Similarly, the symptoms of PPD vary from mom to mom depending on several factors: ease of pregnancy, duration of labor, familial support, number of balloon bouquets received, and access to chocolate. The most common symptoms are:

* Frequent crying
* Lethargy
* Insomnia
* Irritability

THE SYMPTOMS

FREQUENT CRYING

The mother with PPD will cry anywhere from three to seventy-five times a day. This is a biochemical reaction caused by a postnatal hormonal plunge not unlike the plummet of drunken fraternity boys bungee-jumping off a bridge. With no provocation whatsoever, a new mother will weep uncontrollably at anything:

* *The Wonder Years* reruns
* Scratchy toilet paper
* Puppies
* John Denver songs
* Low-fat salad dressing
* *Andy Griffith* reruns
* Spilled milk

LETHARGY

While it is perfectly normal to feel a lack of energy after

passing an eight-pound baby through an opening the size of the neck of a ketchup bottle, women with PPD will act especially sluggish, listless, and uninterested. This alone should not be cause for alarm unless the patient shows a lack of interest in the one thing vital to her survival: shopping.

Theresa K., a twenty-nine-year-old mother of two, recalls how a bout with PPD left her devastatingly detached from outlet malls.

Prior to the birth of my first child, I was an outlet diva. I could easily go all day, covering three hundred miles at a sweep. Mikasa clerks knew me by name. The Liz Claiborne people knew my colors and favorite styles. But after delivery, I was so blue. So out of sorts. The baby wasn't sleeping and my horny husband wouldn't leave me alone. Friends stopped calling. My mother was very concerned. It finally took a closeout sale at the Polo outlet to bring me around—75 percent off everything in the store. Thank God for Ralph Lauren. I really owe him my life. If I have one bit of advice to give to postpartum women, it's this: If you can't get excited by a 40 percent discount, seek professional help immediately.

INSOMNIA

A new mother is required to survive on an infinitesimal amount of sleep. Her inner clock is constantly out of sync as day blurs into night and night blurs into . . . more night. Her nerves are raw and she becomes, literally, "too tired to sleep." She tries everything: warm milk, counting sheep, the History Channel. Nothing works. Ironically, when she does manage to drift off for an hour or two, she is inevitably jostled awake by one of the following:

* Baby's cry
* Aching breasts
* Horny husband

She takes some comfort in the fact that the crying and aching will subside with time. But the realization that her husband's horniness will never, ever wane sends her deeper and deeper into a funk.

IRRITABILITY

New mothers tend to be a bit testy. This is understandable and expected. Remember, their hormones are fluctuating like the Dow-Jones industrial average. But PPD takes hypersensitivity to new heights. Any incident, no matter how seemingly trivial, can trigger rage on a par with Joan Crawford's over the Wire Hangers Incident. There is no limit to the number of things that can launch the fury, but here is a short list:

Sounds . . . smells . . . spills . . . phone solicitors . . . junk mail . . . unsolicited advice . . . *Sports Illustrated* swimsuit edition . . . Kathie Lee Gifford . . . unmade beds . . . crickets . . . Donny and Marie . . . panty hose . . . horny husbands . . . litter boxes . . . nursing bras . . . voice mail . . . spit-up . . . Montel Williams . . . aluminum foil . . . Weight Watchers ads . . . laundry . . . construction zones . . . cottage cheese . . . Richard Simmons . . . pimples . . . bugs . . . Victoria Principal . . . radio interference . . . *The Real World* . . . drippy faucets . . . crabgrass . . . mothers-in-law . . . Jewel . . . chalky deodorant . . . aftershave lotion . . . Rush Limbaugh . . . razor nicks . . . bad hair . . . birds . . . sunlight.

THE TREATMENT

Incidence of Postpartum Depression has increased exponentially as hospitals, bowing to pressure from insurance companies, have shortened postnatal stays from the traditional five to seven days to one to two days. Today, new mothers are released from the hospital with their hormones raging, unprepared for the stresses ahead. In light of this, private postnatal clinics have opened for new mothers desiring longer-term care. These clinics offer a minimum of thirty-day stays with flattering lighting, skinny mirrors, and a no-kids visitors policy.

CHAPTER 16

TOO MUCH INFORMATION SYNDROME

TMIS

THE FACTS

In the '50s, women didn't talk à lot. *Yes, dear. Don't touch. Meat loaf or chicken? You'll poke an eye out. Coffee? Stop it or you'll go blind. On the rocks.* That was pretty much it. Enter women's lib and the consciousness-raising groups of the '60s and '70s. Suddenly, menfolk were encouraged to go bowling. Kids were sent to their rooms. Women gathered braless in shag-carpeted dens just to talk. And talk they did. About anything and *everything*:

- Politics
- Cramps
- Equal work for equal pay
- Orgasms (or lack thereof)
- Religion
- Vaginas
- Labor unions
- Stretch marks
- The latest macramé knots

Initially, these forums were good for the soul and the collective consciousness of womankind. Soon, women were demanding the same openness from men. "You don't communicate" became the number one complaint of wives and girlfriends. Faced with the terrifying prospect of their partners withholding sex, men made a feeble attempt to express themselves with phrases like: "I'm getting in touch with my feminine side," "I feel your pain," and "You want me to stroke your what?" Of course, they failed miserably. Women were forced, once again, to talk amongst themselves.

Now some women have reached a level of personal expression beyond the limits of normal human discourse. Way beyond. This phenomenon is called **Too Much Information Syndrome (TMIS),** or **Oversharing.**

Sometimes called "loose lips" or, in its acute form, "diarrhea of the mouth," TMIS is an inability to curb the tongue when common sense and propriety dictate discretion. Victims of TMIS will share the most intimate details of their lives with anybody, anywhere. Experts in the field estimate that one out of every two women experiences episodes of TMIS, while 40 percent of those are chronic oversharers. (These extreme cases generally fall into three groups: waitresses, celebrities, and the woman sitting next to you on the plane.) Women with TMIS will overshare on any topic, but the most common are:

* Medical procedures
* Their children
* Sex

THE SYMPTOMS

MEDICAL PROCEDURES

If there is one question you should never ask a TMIS sufferer, it's:

"How are you?"

This is a grave mistake because, due to a glitch in the neurotransmitting electromagnetic goo of the brain's full-

frontal lobe connecting her auditory canal, the oversharer
does not hear:

"How are you?"

Instead, she hears:
"Tell me—in excruciatingly tedious detail—
all about yourself and your family, including your
pets. Don't hold anything back. I have all day."

In response, the woman with TMIS goes into no-
holds-barred, uncensored, way-too-much-information-
for the-grocery-store mode with an answer like:

*Heavy sigh. "Well, I'm better now that the yeast infection
has cleared up. That was no fun. But what was I gonna do? Not
take antibiotics for a sinus infection? With phlegm like I had? It
was mucus city for two weeks. Coughing and hacking and spitting up green stuff. Of course, that was nothing compared to
Jamie's diarrhea. I tell ya, I gagged a maggot getting that stool
sample out of the toilet. And now that Jim's been laid off, he just
can't get it up anymore . . ."*

THEIR CHILDREN

It is sometimes difficult to distinguish between the proud
mother who just wants to share her child's latest accom-

plishment and the TMIS mom, sometimes referred to as
the Mother from Hell. The table below will help you tell
the difference:

Proud Mother	***Mother from Hell***
Has latest school picture in wallet	Carries family scrapbooks in her purse
Knows child's GPA	Has memorized every grade he ever got in every subject since kindergarten
Introduces child to guests at party	Makes child perform thirty-minute recital of voice, piano, and baton twirling followed by a recitation of the Gettysburg Address
When asked, "How are the kids?" answers, "Great. Still playing ball!"	When asked, "How are the kids?" answers with their box scores for the entire season.

Mothers with TMIS are particularly troublesome at parent–teacher conferences, when oversharing can push teachers and other parents over the edge. An incident at Holy Smoke Catholic High School in Camden, Florida, provides a cautionary example. There, a TMIS-afflicted mother was physically removed from a chemistry lab after monopolizing the teacher's time for over seventy minutes. An angry mob of parents carried her off and locked her in an empty gym locker. The custodian found her the next morning, tired and stiff, but still talking.

SEX

Thanks to Masters and Johnson and Madonna, sexuality has come a long way since the pent-up '50s. Sex has come out of the closet, down the hall, out the front door, onto the freeway, down the exit ramp, and right into the cubicle next to yours. Every work environment in the free world has a TMIS-stricken woman who overshares about sex. You know the one. The gal who buys her business suits from the Victoria's Secret catalog. She's the babe with the stiletto heels, ankle bracelet, and a rose tattooed on her cleavage. And this isn't the sex talk you remember from the girls bathroom in junior high. This requires a whole new vocabulary, available only on the Internet.

But unlike other oversharers, whose mindless babble

sends their audience into the zombie zone, when *this* woman talks—people listen! And the more people listen, the more she feels compelled to share. Amy Jo, a twenty-nine-year-old accounts payable clerk from San Antonio, Texas, remembers an encounter with such a woman in the company lounge:

I was just sitting down with my Diet Coke for my afternoon break. There were a couple of gals from Traffic sitting at the next table fixated on this girl, Jeannine, from Sales. I couldn't hear everything she was saying, but every now and then, I'd catch a phrase or two like "hot, dripping wax" and "handcuffs and honey." By the time my coffee break was over, there were fifty-four people at Jeannine's table. Some were taking notes.

So how does one know if a person is afflicted with chronic TMIS? The Joan Rivers "Thank You for Not Sharing" Institute in Concord, California, recently published a pamphlet containing the following warning signs:

EXCESSIVE THIRST OR DRY MOUTH

Women with TMIS suffer from a shortage of saliva, caused by incessant talking. This condition, commonly called "cotton mouth," can cause secondary symptoms like chapped lips, bad breath and a craving for Gatorade.

THREE-DIGIT PHONE BILLS

The telephone is an oversharer's most dangerous enabler. TMIS victims are on the phone constantly. With the proliferation of new services like call waiting and call return— not to mention cell phones, pagers, and fax machines— $500 to $800 phone bills are a common result.

CYBERSHARING

The Internet has provided TMIS patients a multitude of venues for oversharing: chat rooms, cybercams, and, worst of all, the personal Web page. Chat rooms are crowded with TMIS suffers sharing their most intimate thoughts on a variety of important subjects like:

* Marriage
* Divorce
* Lipton Soup recipes
* The mini- vs. maxi-pad debate

Savvy chatters express their opinions and emotions using special symbols like:

$$:) \ = \ \text{Happy}$$
$$: (\ = \ \text{Sad}$$
$$; - Q \ !! \ = \ \text{I'd kill for a cigarette}$$

The proliferation of personal Web pages proves the extent to which TMIS has spread in the country. Habitual oversharers post their latest family photos and news, encouraging friends and family to "visit our site often and see how Bobby Jr. keeps growin' like a weed!"

Cybercam sites provide live video images of the over-sharer's every move, twenty-four hours a day. The most delusional TMIS sufferers believe the average cybersurfer has nothing better to do than watch women brushing their teeth, doing the dishes, vacuuming, painting their toenails, and watching Springer. Unfortunately, they are right.

AVERAGE TIME AT A DRIVE-THROUGH WINDOW: TWENTY-FIVE MINUTES

It is physically impossible for an oversharer to proceed through a drive-through lane at a fast-food restaurant in less than fifteen minutes. Why? Well, think of all the things there are to discuss: Do you want cheese with that? How many ketchups? Cream in your coffee? Supersize or regular? Cup holder or no? Once the oversharer arrives at the pickup window, she's compelled to review her choices and explain *why* she chose cheese, three ketchups, no cream but sugar, regular, and a cup holder. She can't help it.

SPEAKING IN DIALOGUES

A woman suffering from TMIS will tell stories as if scripted in a play or movie. Typically, she will play all the parts, complete with voice changes, accents, and gestures:

So I go, "That's not the haircut that was in the picture!"

And he goes, "There's no way you're gonna look like Jennifer Aniston. I'm not a magician."

And I go, "Then why didn't you tell me that before you started cutting."

And he goes, "I did tell you. You didn't listen."

And I go, "Did not!"

And he goes, "Did too!"

And I go, "Listen, Marco. I'm not going to pay for this butcher job and you can't make me."

And he goes, "Oh, yeah!"

And I go, "Yeah."

Even if the woman is interrupted and asked to cut to the chase because, say, her hair is on fire, she will immediately pick up the conversation, verbatim, untill the bitter end . . .

So I go, "Yeah! And another thing. That Claire Danes cut you gave me last year sucked! Not once has anybody said I looked just like her!"

And he goes, "Bitter, party of one . . . your table is ready! Hel-lo!"

And I go . . .

THE TREATMENT

Unfortunately, a cure for TMIS has yet to be discovered. The most effective treatment, to date, is a revolutionary idea conceived by Dr. Barrett Vanderklemption at a conference of the American Association of Too Much Information Syndrome Specialists in Washington, D.C. In presenting his groundbreaking paper to an audience of his peers and two hundred chronic oversharers, Dr. Vanderklemption said:

"For God's sake, shut up!"

CHAPTER 17

DIET
DELIRIUM

(DD)

THE FACTS

The Baroque period (1600–1790 A.D.) was the last real heyday for chunky gals. Flemish-born artist Peter Paul Rubens made overnight celebrities of the pudgy ladies he put in his paintings—sprawling naked on chaises, drinking wine, munching grapes with wild abandon. Fat was in. Gluttony was golden. And broads with thunder thighs were hot, hot, hot!

But all good things must come to an end, and so, too, did the era of the zaftig woman. Soon, the Impressionists were in vogue and Rubenesque models were given an ultimatum: Shape up or lose your union card! Suddenly, women embarked on frantic campaigns to battle the bulge. Kumquat diets, fortnight fasts, and workout racks became all the rage. This was the beginning of the global epidemic known as **Diet Delirium,** sometimes referred to as **DD.**

The Association of Overweight Chain-Smoking Physicians (AOCSP) defines Diet Delirium as "the uncontrollable urge to try any new weight-loss gimmick on the market—no matter how weird, expensive, or torturous."

Take this quiz to determine if *you* are at risk for DD:

1. You will find the following books on my shelves at home:
    A. *The Complete Scarsdale Medical Diet, The Zone, Weight Watchers, Dr. Atkins' New Diet Revolution, Protein Power,* Oprah Winfrey's *Make the Connection*
    B. All of the above *plus Suzanne Somers' Get Skinny on Fabulous Foods, Sugar Busters, The Beverly Hills Diet, The Rotation Diet*
    C. All of the above *plus* Delta Burke's *Ho-Ho Diet, Purge with Calista,* Dr. Joyce Brothers's *Gorging Without Guilt,* Dr. Laura's *Ten Stupid Things Women Eat to Mess Up Their Thighs*
    D. *Fat Is a Feminist Issue* and *Moby-Dick*

2. If you unlocked my attic right now, you would find:

    A. A NordicTrack

    B. A NordicTrack, treadmill, and rowing machine

    C. A NordicTrack, treadmill, rowing machine, StairMaster, Thighmaster, three sets of dumbells, eight exercise videos, and a pair of inversion boots

    D. Richard Simmons

3. I use my stationary bike:

    A. Daily

    B. Weekly

    C. Monthly

    D. To dry my panty hose

4. The last diet I was on lasted:

    A. Six weeks

    B. Six days

    C. Six hours

    D. An entire bite

How to score:

If you circled mostly A's, you have a *low to moderate risk* for developing Diet Delirium. Reward yourself with a Diet Coke.

If you circled mostly B's, you have a *moderate to high risk*. Consume three Cheez-Its and a snickerdoodle. You'll get over it.

If you answered mostly C's, you are in the *high to over-the-top* risk category. Snarf a box of Ring-Dings ASAP.

If all of your answers were 'D', go straight for the Ben & Jerry's. (Let's face it, you were halfway there anyway.)

Women afflicted with DD fall into four categories:

❋ The Collector
❋ The Crash and Burner
❋ The Fad Follower
❋ The Virtual Dieter

THE SYMPTOMS

THE COLLECTOR

The woman ailing from Diet Delirium is compelled to collect every diet book, exercise gadget, and videotape on the market in hopes that *one* of them will provide the results she is looking for—a body like Elle McPherson's in twenty-four hours or less. In this woman's closet, you will find dozens of books, tapes, and pieces of equipment—many of them still shrink-wrapped in cellophane. *Collectors should take every precaution to avoid infomercials and home-shopping networks, such as QVC.* In fact, after making a diagnosis of DD, many physicians will prescribe immediate disconnection of cable TV.

THE CRASH AND BURNER (C&B)

This is the woman who, with five days to go before the Party of the Year, will starve herself mercilessly in hopes of squeezing into the size-eight dress she bought six months ago for "motivation" to lose weight. Typically, this woman is at least a size twelve. She proceeds to deprive herself of solids, drinking only water with lemon and an occasional Tab. She exercises seven times a day, wearing rubber shorts to expedite perspiration and weighing herself after each workout. After five excruciating days, she is eight pounds lighter but still a full size shy of her goal. On the afternoon of the event, she staggers to the mall crazed with hunger and buys the first cocktail dress she can zip up. At the Party of the Year, she plants herself next to the buffet table with a split of champagne and stuffs down every morsel of food that isn't hot-glued to the centerpiece.

THE FAD FOLLOWER

Fad diets are irresistible to women with DD . . . and the more bizarre, the better. Each week, new fads scream at these defenseless grocery shoppers from the covers of the tabloids:

NEW!! CHER & CHASTITY'S GAY PRIDE DIET—
ALL THE RAINBOW SHERBET YOU CAN EAT!!!

ALIEN DIET GIVES 45-LB. NEWBORN SLEEK NEW LOOK!!!
LOSE 5 POUNDS A DAY ON MONICA LEWINSKY'S
CIGAR DIET!!

Medical experts warn against fad diets, as they tend to be nutritionally unbalanced, calorie-deficient, and damaging to your social life. Florence, a twenty-eight-year-old actress, describes how a popular diet almost destroyed her career and ended her relationship:

I had about ten pounds to lose before an audition and somebody told me about this Cabbage Soup Diet. I thought, "What the hell? I can eat anything for two weeks!" I made gallons of the stuff, with lots of onions, peppers, and fourteen heads of cabbage . . . seasoned to taste, of course. Well, it worked like a charm . . . except for one little problem. I was repeating like an AK-47! My boyfriend moved out, saying he wanted to put more "space between us . . . like ten city blocks." Friends started calling me Flatulence Flo. But the final blow, so to speak, came at the audition. I was doing Juliet's death scene: "Oh happy dagger . . . this is thy sheath; there rust, and let me die." I fell on the sword, collapsing on Romeo's body. The theater was dead quiet . . . until I let loose the loudest gaseous fanfare the world has ever heard. Needless to say, I didn't get the part. But the director did cast me in his next show: Inherit the Wind.

THE VIRTUAL DIETER

This DD victim is the woman who claims to be dieting constantly but eats whatever she wants without an inkling of guilt. This requires a complex psychological process of rationalization in which the woman comes to *believe* certain rules of acceptable diet exemptions:

1. Food that you eat off other people's plates, especially children's, has no calories. It is "borrowed" food and thus can be "returned." That is why you can finish your kids' desserts every night without gaining a pound.

2. Food eaten on the run—in the car or on foot—has no calories. "On the run" is the equivalent of "running," which burns up to eight hundred calories per hour, thus negating your intake and accelerating your metabolism for the rest of the day.

3. Hot food that gets cold loses its calories, and they will not be regained when it is reheated, if a microwave is used.

4. If you are eating food sold to you by nonprofit organizations like the Girl Scouts or Little League baseball teams, you may deduct 50 percent of the calories as a charitable donation.

5. Food from the children's menu has 40 percent fewer calories than the same food on the regular menu because it costs 40 percent less. This is why you can steal food off your kids' plates when they're not looking and not gain a pound.

6. If you are on a business trip with a $100-a-day meal allowance, you may deduct up to $100 worth of calories per diem, excluding liquor.

7. Silly or improbable food, like cheese in a can, has no calories because who takes food like that seriously, anyway?

THE TREATMENT

Until modern society stops worshiping buns and abs of steel and starts finding the beauty hidden within the folds of dimpled thighs and tummies, there is little hope for a permanent cure of Diet Delirium. For now, the best treatment seems to be the "DD patch," which, when affixed to the skin on the second stomach roll below the navel, can stave off cravings for celery, soda water, and Tae-Bo videos . . . at least temporarily.

CHAPTER 18

EMPTY NEST SYNDROME

(ENS)

THE FACTS

A mother's job is to raise her child to be independent. Under normal conditions, and not including jail time or military service, this is an eighteen- to twenty-two-year process. Mom stops cutting his meat, wiping his bottom, combing her hair, and doing her laundry. The kid grows up, moves out, makes his own living, and, God willing, sends a potted plant or cheap cologne within ten days of Mom's birthday. It's the universal exit strategy. But in some cases, when the child finally leaves the nest . . . Mom freaks out. Experts have identified this response as **Empty Nest Syndrome,** or **ENS.**

There are two types of ENS sufferers:

1. ENS-Type D: Mothers who *dread* the empty nest
2. ENS-Type CW: Moms who *can't wait* for the brats to go

Each type comes with its own distinct set of symptoms, but syndromes can overlap or alternate at anytime.

THE SYMPTOMS

ENS-TYPE D: DREADING THE EMPTY NEST

ENS-D is a form of separation anxiety, and victims will often exhibit warning signs early in the child's life. The most common indicator is uncontrollable sobbing. Mothers predisposed to ENS-D will spontaneously burst into tears on any occasion remotely representing a milestone in the child's life:

* First haircut
* Kindergarten graduation
* First period
* First pimple

* First day of Driver's Ed
* Last day of Driver's Ed (not for the same reason)

Another common early warning sign is excessive waving. Women who are prone to ENS-D cannot say good-bye to their child without waving wildly for extraordinarily long periods of time. This is typically the mother who is still waving three minutes after the school bus pulls away from the curb. In extreme cases, the woman attempts to prolong the child's departure by running alongside the bus, train, or plane. This behavior can be dangerous and is not recommended.

Angela, twenty-nine, an ENS-D sufferer from San Jose, California, recounts a near-death experience while waving:

I was sending Tommy off to day camp. He'd never ridden in a school bus before and he was so excited. I told him to give a signal out the window when he found his seat, but he got distracted. I started waving. You know, just to get his attention? The bus pulled away and I started running next to it. Jogging at first, then into a full sprint. Pretty soon, all the kids were looking at me, laughing and pointing. All except Tommy. I ran faster and started leaping up to look in the windows. I didn't notice that the bus was slowing down. Suddenly, this giant stop sign swung out from the bus, smacked me in the face, and knocked me flat! The bus driver dropped me off at the emergency room. It was on the way. Tommy didn't speak to me for a week.

Other early warning signs of ENS-D include:
* Inability to pack a child for a slumber party without tearing up
* Leaving "Hurry home!" notes in school lunches
* Refusing to leave on Visiting Day at camp

If early warning signs are ignored, a predisposed mother can develop a serious ENS disorder. By the time the child is of legal age, the symptoms will have become far more severe. Scientists studying ENS-D victims at the Joan Crawford Institute for the Maternally Impaired say patients experience symptoms similar to those of the crack addict denied a fix.

Women in the throes of ENS withdrawal say they start craving things they swore they'd never miss:
* 2:00 A.M. phone calls from the police
* Dirty underwear on the banister
* Body glitter in the sink
* Tire tracks through the yard
* Toilet-seat splatters
* MTV
* Cap'n Crunch in the carpet

The mother deprived of the above will sit for long periods of time, motionless from lack of stimuli. To cope with their depression and anxiety, some women take desperate measures to feel normal again. Geneva, a forty-six-year-old empty-nester from Seattle, shares her feelings after her youngest son left home the first time:

After Slug moved out, I'd wander up to his old room and just sit on his futon, staring at his Save the Hemp posters and moldy cereal bowls. I'd find myself gazing longingly at the teenage pan-handlers that hang out downtown. One looked so much like Slug, I offered him twenty bucks to come home with me, play grunge music at deafening decibel levels, and let me yell at him about his hair for a while. By the time I realized I was just looking for a surrogate son, the kid had called the cops on me.

ENS-TYPE CW: CAN'T WAIT FOR THE BRATS TO GO

On the flip side of this mysterious syndrome are the women who *eagerly anticipate* the day when the last child leaves the nest. These women live "in the closet," since society tends to frown on mothers who can't wait to ditch their kids. Contrary to popular belief, these women are not cold and heartless. They're just tired of sharing. Their motives include:

* Converting that smelly bedroom to one of those "all about me" rooms Oprah is always talking about
* Planning a garage sale for the day after the kid moves out
* Reclaiming their refrigerators, clothes, CDs, and dishes

To that end, these women will go to great lengths to expedite the child's exit from the nest. Delores, a fifty-year-old mother of three daughters, writes:

When my youngest, Astrid, hit puberty I secretly began sending away for college brochures. It wasn't that I didn't love her. I just wanted my bathroom back. On her sixteenth birthday, I presented her with a stack of university brochures, alphabetized, cataloged, and prioritized according to geographic location and chances of getting in based on her current GPA. I signed her up for SAT and ACT tests, had her résumé professionally done, secured letters of recommendation, the works. On her eighteenth birthday, she announced she was planning to matriculate at the local cosmetology school and would be living at home to save money. I grieve for the bathroom I lost, but my nails have never looked better.

Like Delores, mothers with ENS-CW tend to rush the child's departure, forcing the child to grow up earlier than he should. Jeannie, a forty-four-year-old mother of one, confesses:

On the first day of college enrollment, I woke Joey up early for the five-hour drive to the state university. He was still groggy from a party the night before, but the car had been packed for days. I told him to hop in the back and he could sleep all the way. When we reached the residence hall, I got his key and carried his stuff to his room. He seemed a bit dazed, but his dad and I took care of everything—unpacking him, hooking up the computer and stereo, making his bunk bed. As I gave him a kiss good-bye—eager to get home to my new sewing room—his eyes welled up with tears. "What's wrong?" I said. "You've never been homesick before!" He looked at me with pain in his eyes and said, "But Mom, I still have one more year of high school!"

THE TREATMENT

There is no cure for Empty Nest Syndrome. No vaccine. No panacea. But sufferers can take comfort in the fact that, in 82 percent of all cases, ENS is a temporary condition. Just when you adjust to your new life without the kids, they come back. And this time, they have brats of their own.

CHAPTER 19

MY MOTHER, MYSELF DISEASE

(MMMD)

THE FACTS

In the beginning there was Eve. Eve had two sons, Cain and Abel, who had earned quite a reputation around Paradise for their good-cop–bad-cop routines. Not quite so well known was Eve's daughter, Sheila. While her brothers bickered over the family sheep, Sheila stayed home to work at her mother's side. As a result, Sheila became an expert at shearing, spinning wool, and cooking a mean lamb stew . . . just like her mom.

Soon, Sheila noticed she was becoming more like Eve than she ever desired—chatting with serpents, sneaking forbidden fruits, wearing last year's fig leaf. One day, while preparing a ewe for slaughter, she heard herself utter one of Eve's signature sayings:

"Don't look at me in that tone of voice!"

Mortified, Sheila banished herself from the family and ran off with a guy named Noah. This was the first recorded case of **MMMD,** or **My Mother, Myself Disease.**

MMMD is caused by the inner conflict that arises when you realize:

1. your mother drives you crazier than any human being on earth, and
2. you are becoming more like her every day.

Take this quiz to see if you might be suffering from MMMD:

1. When driving across town, I like to:
    A. See how far I can go without changing lanes
    B. Test my brakes every tenth of a mile
    C. Listen to *Prairie Home Companion*
2. When my ten-year-old has a glob of ketchup on his face, I:

A. Tell him to go to the bathroom and wash it off before it gets on his shirt

B. Dip a paper napkin in a glass of ice water and wipe it off myself

C. Lick my thumb and rub his cheek with my saliva until he swears off ketchup for the rest of his life

3. In the parking lot at the mall, I routinely:

A. Drive in circles until I find a parking spot on the end of the row

B. Take up two parking spaces

C. Follow slowly behind shoppers as they walk to their cars to see if they have a spot on the end of the row.

If you answered A, B, or C to any of the above questions, you may already suffer from My Mother, Myself Disease.

Symptoms of MMMD include:

* Motherspeak
* Body morph
* Doling out unsolicited advice
* Co-dependent decision making
* Maternal ESP (when the mother knows you've done something—even from one thousand miles away)
* Sensible shoes

THE SYMPTOMS

MOTHERSPEAK

One of the earliest warning signs of MMMD is hearing yourself say those words you swore you'd *never* say as long as you lived:

* ❋ Eat before it gets cold!
* ❋ Don't pick, it'll get infected.
* ❋ Take that out of your mouth. You don't know where it's been.
* ❋ Because I said so, that's why!
* ❋ Not in your good clothes.
* ❋ Yoo-hoo!

Eventually, your voice starts sounding exactly like your mother's. Your father finds it impossible to differentiate between your voices when you phone. Sometimes, before you can identify yourself, he starts talking dirty: "Hurry home, Mommy—Daddy needs a spanking." Some women find this disturbingly Freudian and go immediately into therapy.

BODY MORPH

Between the ages of thirty and forty-five, a woman will wake up and discover that her body has become, for better or for worse, exactly like her mother's. From wagging underarms to varicose veins, liver spots to turkey neck ... a mother's physical legacy is the gift that keeps on giving. That's why when someone tells a woman, "You're just like your mother!" she doesn't know whether to say "Thank you" or "Go suck an egg."

DOLING OUT UNSOLICITED ADVICE

An MMMD-afflicted woman feels compelled to offer advice to everyone—children, co-workers, perfect strangers. This is especially true when the advice concerns health matters or household hints. Elena, a thirty-four-year-old district attorney, recalls an MMMD moment on an elevator:

I was on my way to the fiftieth floor with a couple of attorneys I didn't know. One of them had a terrible cough. He couldn't stop hacking. I just blurted out, "You know, a little lemon and honey would do the trick for that nagging cough." He thanked me and, since we were just at the thirty-second floor, I turned to the other guy and said, "A little club soda will take that marinara-sauce stain right out." "Really?" he asked. By the time we reached fifty, I'd given the first guy all my tissues and was brushing the lint off the other one's jacket. They were okay with it, but I when I realized what I had done, I got so dizzy I had to sit down.

CO-DEPENDENT DECISION MAKING

One of the most puzzling aspects of MMMD is the tendency for independent, successful women to consult their mothers before making decisions, large or small. Tricia L., thirty-nine, CEO of her own textile-design company, confesses:

I oversee a staff of 150 people and a $20 million annual budget. I have an MBA from Brown, a mortgage, and a 401K. And yet, before I can purchase a dining room set, a pair of shoes, or a $15 lipstick . . . I have to call my mom. I'll call her directly from the store, describing in great detail the item I'm considering. She gives the same advice every time: "If it's too trendy, you'll get tired of it." I've tried to go it alone, but I always end up buying something stupid, like palazzo pants.

MATERNAL ESP

According to scientific polls conducted by the Dionne Warwick Institute of Psychic Phenomenon in San Jose, about half of all Americans say they believe in extrasensory perception. The other half aren't sure but want to take advantage of the first free reading. But a significant 95.2 percent of those surveyed claimed to believe in maternal ESP—the ability of a mother to read minds, see through phone lines, and "smell trouble."

There are three varieties of maternal ESP:

❊ Telepathy (mind-to-mind communication): The mother sends thoughts to the child like "Don't even *think* about borrowing my car" or "I am so disappointed in you."

❊ Clairvoyance (perceiving remote events): Such as when the mother senses that an adult, unmarried daughter didn't sleep in her own bed the night before.

❊ Precognition, or perceiving future events: Such as "If you don't come for Thanksgiving, something terrible will happen, like your father getting a goiter."

SENSIBLE SHOES

Another mysterious manifestation of MMMD is the woman's sudden desire for sensible shoes. This generally occurs between the ages of thirty and forty—earlier for waitresses, nurses, and postal workers. At this time, a woman will permanently switch from heels to flats, adopting her mother's dress code of appropriate footwear.

CHAPTER 20

CAN'T REMEMBER SQUAT

(CRS)

THE FACTS

The female brain is the most powerful, efficient, and versatile of all the organs in the human body, including the male organs. Yes, even that one. With the capacity to perform more functions simultaneously than a NASA supercomputer, a woman's brain can tackle innumerable tasks at the same time:

* Critical decision making: *Paper or plastic?*
* Complex algebraic calculations: *If one truffle has 130 calories and one aerobics class burns 600 calories*

per hour, how many trips to the gym will it take to work off a dozen amaretto cremes?

✻ Intricate hand-eye coordination: *French-braiding.*

✻ Existential thought: *I bloat, therefore I am.*

But the most impressive characteristic of the female brain is its complex network of *memory circuits.* A woman experiences life through her senses: sights, sounds, feelings, tastes, smells, and the sixth "flight or fight" sense that protects her from the perfume squirters at Macy's.

These sensory impulses are transmitted and stored in brain "centers," sometimes referred to as "memory banks." Each "bank" holds "deposits," or "reserves," of information, which she can "withdraw" at any time. But as a woman ages, she occasionally forgets to "balance" her brain's "checkbook," thus depleting her "reserves" and forcing the memory bank to close her "account" for "insufficient funds." When this happens, a woman may experience a syndrome called **CRS,** or **Can't Remember Squat.**

CRS is a mysterious disorder that compromises a woman's short-term memory while leaving long-term memories (such as the first names of the entire Partridge family) virtually intact. The condition has baffled the medical community for years, as scientists struggle to explain why a woman can vividly recall:

* what she wore to a Three Dog Night concert in
  seventh grade;
* the birthdays of all her old boyfriends;
* every *I Love Lucy* episode;
* phone numbers from thirty years ago;
* the lyrics to every Joni Mitchell song ever written . . .

and yet drive for miles before realizing she left her purse
on top of the car.

Can't Remember Squat is a disease that progresses in
three stages, determined by the declining degrees of a
woman's mind:

* Stage One: Going
* Stage Two: Going
* Stage Three: Gone!

THE SYMPTOMS

STAGE ONE: GOING

The first phase of CRS commonly occurs in women
around the age of thirty, more or less depending on the
number of kids, husbands, and joints smoked in college.
Early warning signs include:

* Forgetting names of acquaintances

* Misplacing items like car keys and the remote control
* Arriving fifteen minutes late for doctor's appointments
* Inability to locate your car in the airport parking lot

Most women attribute these lapses to the stress of daily life, being preoccupied, or simply not paying attention. And while the symptoms are mild and do not warrant treatment, a woman in Stage One should still be cautious and avoid gas appliances.

STAGE TWO: GOING

Around the age of forty, a woman will notice more significant memory lapses, including:

* Forgetting the names of co-workers or friends
* Misplacing items like dinner
* Arriving a week late for doctor's appointments
* Inability to locate car in the office parking garage

These symptoms can be inconvenient and annoying but, in most cases, are not a cause for alarm . . . unless, of course, the misplaced dinner is fish.

STAGE THREE: GONE

In the most advanced stage, CRS will cause one or more of the following behaviors:

* ❋ Forgetting the name of the person in bed next to you
* ❋ Misplacing items like the family cat or youngest child
* ❋ Arriving a year late or early for a doctor's appointment
* ❋ Inability to locate your car in your own garage

At this stage, intervention is *highly* recommended.

COPING

A woman with CRS will go to great lengths to hide her affliction from friends and family. Employing extreme and sometimes bizarre strategies, she desperately tries to keep herself on track. Some of the most common coping mechanisms are:

1. NAME TAGS

CRS victims have a difficult time remembering names. That's why some women literally leap for joy when they spy the name-tag table at a party or meeting. By the same token, there are those who experience profound anxiety when name tags are not supplied at a function. Diana C., forty-six, known as "the tag lady of Cincinnati," carries a large supply of "Hi, My Name is . . ." badges everywhere she goes, just in case:

You never know when you're going to be in a situation where you need name tags—PTA meetings, weddings, elevators. So, I just make a point of placing a name tag on each and every person I come in contact with. That way, there's no chance of embarrassment. No awkward introductions like "And you are . . .?" It's kind of expensive, of course, especially at football games . . . but once I slap the tags on, people really like 'em . . . especially the women.

2. LISTS

One of the most helpful tools used by women with CRS is the "To Do" list. Women who can't remember squat will painstakingly create lists of tasks to accomplish in a day, week, or month. Often, these lists are prioritized with red flags, exclamation points, or codes:

A = Priority one—get it done *now*

B = Important, do this ASAP

C = Pretty important, try not to forget

D = Why bother?

Unfortunately, CRS victims will spend an extraordinary amount of time composing "To Do" lists only to lose them, throw them out with the newspapers, or shred them with the coleslaw.

Another invaluable tool is the "grocery list." *Women with CRS should NEVER go to the supermarket without a list!!!* Police files are full of missing-person reports on women who went to the grocery store without a shopping list . . . and never returned. Without the list as a crutch, the CRS-afflicted woman will wander aimlessly through the store, staring for hours at dairy cases, produce stands, and meat counters, muttering: "Now, what did I come in for?" At closing time, grocers conduct "ditz sweeps," clearing confused female customers from the aisles and ushering them out of the store. This can be dangerous, especially if a woman can't find her car at night.

3. STICKY NOTES

The single most effective weapon in the fight against CRS is the sticky note. Recovering CRS victims will use sticky notes on everything—refrigerators, phones, dashboards, headboards—wherever a gentle reminder is needed. The habit can get out of hand, however, when sticky notes are abused. Margo H., a thirty-nine-year-old mother of four is in recovery from inappropriate sticky-note application:

I was always forgetting which kid had to be where for after-school activities. Sometimes I'd drop Jimmy off at ballet and take Kirsten to wrestling practice. It was embarrassing. Finally, I found a solution. Every morning, I applied sticky notes to the kids' foreheads—like "Tae Kwon Do—4:15." Then when I picked them up in the afternoon, I knew exactly where to take them. It was great for a while, but then the kids started having trouble at school. Bullies called them "Post-it Face." Teachers accused them of passing notes in class. Julie developed an ulcer. Tommy got a rash on his forehead. I spent six weeks in therapy kicking my sticky-note habit. But I must confess, I still stick 'em on the dog. Otherwise, he'd never get fed.

4. THE PLANNER OR DATEBOOK

Another common tactic for battling the symptoms of Can't Remember Squat is the planner or datebook. Research shows that eight out of ten CRS victims have success using planners. However, a significant 78 percent of those will lose their planners within one month of purchase and never recover them.

THE TREATMENT

The brain is like a muscle. It must be exercised to stay fit. Short-term memory specialists at the National Institute for I Forget What have developed a revolutionary program for women with CRS to help keep their minds in shape. The regime includes these daily exercises:

* Deep breathing
* Reciting the alphabet backward
* Verbal self-reminders ("I am going to the refrigerator for *butter*"; "I am taking my *pills* for the day")
* Flash-card affirmations ("I will remember where I parked"; "I will not leave Jonathan at McDonald's"; "I will take the pot roast out of the pan *before* I put it in the dishwasher")

Since CRS cannot be cured completely, a victim may still experience episodes of anxiety ... especially when something valuable is misplaced, like a toddler in an expensive stroller. In these instances, biofeedback is recommended. The victim should stop, breathe deeply, and apply pressure to the top of her head with both hands for five minutes, or until the fear subsides. Nine out of ten times, the victim will forget what she was upset about and go about her business.